Minority and Gender Differences in Officer Career Progression

Susan D. Hosek

Peter Tiemeyer

Rebecca Kilburn

Debra A. Strong

Selika Ducksworth

Reginald Ray

Prepared for the
Office of the Secretary of Defense

National Defense Research Institute

RAND

The research described in this report was sponsored by the Office of the Secretary of Defense (OSD). The research was conducted in RAND's National Defense Research Institute, a federally funded research and development center supported by the OSD, the Joint Staff, the unified commands, and the defense agencies, Contract DASW01-95-C-0059.

Library of Congress Cataloging-in-Publication Data

Minority and gender differences in officer career progression / Susan D. Hosek ...
[et al.].
    p. cm.
    "MR-1184-OSD."
    Includes bibliographical references.
    ISBN 0-8330-2876-6
    1. United States—Armed Forces—Minorities. 2. United States—Armed
Forces—Officers. I. Hosek, Susan D.

UB417 .R32 2001
355.1'12'0973—dc21

                                                              00-055265

RAND is a nonprofit institution that helps improve policy and decisionmaking through research and analysis. RAND® is a registered trademark. RAND's publications do not necessarily reflect the opinions or policies of its research sponsors.

Published 2001 by RAND
1700 Main Street, P.O. Box 2138, Santa Monica, CA 90407-2138
1200 South Hayes Street, Arlington, VA 22202-5050
201 North Craig Street, Suite 102, Pittsburgh, PA 15213-1516
RAND URL: http://www.rand.org/
To order RAND documents or to obtain additional information,
contact Distribution Services: Telephone: (310) 451-7002;
Fax: (310) 451-6915; Internet: order@rand.org

PREFACE

This report documents research on the career progression of the different minority and gender groups in the officer corps. The research, which was conducted in 1994–1996, contributed to a Department of Defense (DoD) study of equal opportunity in the officer pipeline. Therefore, the officer management policies and procedures described in this report are the ones that were in place at the time the research was conducted. Since that time, numerous changes have been made; important changes are described in the footnotes to the report.

The DoD report, titled *Career Progression of Minority and Women Officers*, was released by the Office of the Under Secretary of Defense for Personnel and Readiness in August 1999. The DoD study was requested by Secretary William Perry in a 1994 memorandum and carried out by the Office of the Under Secretary of Defense for Personnel and Readiness. The Joint Service Equal Opportunity Task Force and the Defense Equal Opportunity Council have continued to address the issues raised in the DoD report and this RAND report.

The RAND project was sponsored by the Assistant Secretary of Defense for Force Management Policy and conducted in the Forces and Resources Policy Center of the National Defense Research Institute (NDRI), a federally funded research and development center sponsored by the Office of the Secretary of Defense, the Joint Staff, the unified commands, and the defense agencies.

CONTENTS

FIGURES

Over the 25 years of the All Volunteer Force, the cohorts of newly commissioned officers have included increasing numbers of minorities and women. Yet future senior officer ranks will only become as diverse as the junior ranks are today if these minority and women officers are retained and promoted.

Between 1967 and 1991, the Pentagon almost quadrupled the representation of minorities in the ranks of its newly commissioned officers to 11 percent. The portion of new officers who were women soared ninefold during that period to 18 percent. Most of the increase occurred in the 1970s. Our study focuses on officers commissioned during this period, 1967–1991, when the junior officer corps became more diverse.

To progress through the officer ranks, individuals need to be promoted and retained between promotions. Our research looks at whether officers obtain the promotions that they need to stay in the military and whether they choose to continue in their careers. We look for patterns of differences between groups of officers defined by both race and gender. When we find differences, we attempt to identify explanations for various promotion and retention outcomes.

RESEARCH APPROACH

We conducted two complementary research efforts to investigate the career progression of minority and female officers. In one effort we analyzed the personnel records of more than 76,000 officers who were commissioned in one of seven years beginning in 1967 and ending in 1991 (1967, 1970, 1977, 1980, 1983, 1987, 1991). These files, provided by the Defense Manpower Data Center, record the race, ethnicity, gender, marital status, commissioning source, and military occupation of each officer. They also allowed us to track how long officers were retained and to determine when they were promoted. We tracked officers through promotion to the O-6 level.

Our study excluded those in the professional ranks—namely, members of the medical corps, lawyers, and chaplains. In most services, those professions have career paths, promotion procedures, and management structures that are distinct from the systems in place for other officers. Using these data we measured retention and promotion by race, ethnicity, and gender at each rank. We also separated the years of service into retention periods—i.e., periods when individual officers made decisions about whether to stay in or depart from the military—and promotion periods—i.e., periods when officers went before promotion boards. We looked at officer career progression as a series of retention and promotion outcomes, each conditional on its predecessor. We classified these outcomes as retention at O-1 rank, promotion to O-2, retention at O-2, promotion to O-3, and so on. In total, we identified nine outcomes that take place between an officer's being promoted to O-2 and receiving a promotion to O-6.

For each of the nine outcomes, we estimated the differences in the fraction retained or promoted between white males and up to three minority and gender groups, depending on sample sizes: black males, other minority males, white women, black women, and other minority women. Our analysis differed from other studies, which typically have estimated differences for whites versus minorities or for men versus women, but not for groups defined by race and gender. We controlled for service, cohort, source of commission, and occupation in those estimates.

Our second research effort involved interviews and focus groups with 233 individuals: 143 midcareer officers, 45 individuals who manage officers, and 45 who select them for promotion. We conducted one-on-one or small group interviews with the career managers and promotion board members in our sample. These sessions were designed to gain information about the career management and promotion system in each military service and the factors linked to a successful career. We also carried out one-on-one interviews with roughly one-quarter of the midcareer officers in our sample; the rest we interviewed in focus groups. Conducted at four major installations from each service, these interviews and focus groups with a cross-section of officers in the middle years of a career were designed to gain information about how the career-management and promotion system is perceived to run.

In general, we selected midcareer participants from each minority and gender group to ensure representation from the full range of commissioning sources and occupational specialties. In the focus groups, we conducted separate sessions for black males, white males, black females, and white females in order to provide an environment in which individuals felt free to express opinions and share experiences. Small numbers made focus groups with other minority groups infeasible.

FINDINGS

In general, we found that women were less likely to reach higher officer ranks (O-4 and above) than were men, but blacks were not significantly less likely to reach higher ranks than were whites. Larger differences emerged when we studied patterns in promotion and retention separately. Black male officers throughout the military generally failed promotions in higher proportions than did their white male counterparts. However, those who were promoted were more likely to stay until the next promotion point. Black male officers were 29 percent more likely to fail promotions than were their white male counterparts but were 20 percent more likely to stay in the military during retention windows. These promotion and retention differences were offsetting, so overall, black and white male officers had essentially the same chance of reaching the career stage at O-4. Combining promotion and retention rates, we found that 37 percent of white men and 36 percent of black men made it to the O-4 rank.

White female officers, in contrast, received promotions in only slightly lower proportions than did white males, but they left the military at earlier career stages, thereby reducing the size of the pool of those remaining eligible for promotion. Compared to white men, white women were only 7 percent more likely to fail promotions, but they were 14 percent more likely to leave during retention periods. The fraction reaching O-4 rank was only 30 percent, substantially below the fraction of white male officers.

Black females showed tendencies both to fail promotion and to leave military service early in their careers. Compared again to white males, they were 39 percent more likely to fail promotion and 14 percent less likely to leave during retention windows. About as many black women as white women reached O-4 rank (31 percent).

Retention and promotion results for other minority groups are limited due to small sample sizes. However, they generally resembled the results for black officers.

Questions arising from these tendencies—Why were blacks less likely to receive promotions? Why were women more likely to leave the military during retention periods?—motivated our interviews and focus groups with midcareer officers. The discussions in these sessions revealed different perceptions about the career experiences of white males compared to black males or black and white females. Despite these differences, almost all officers agreed that promotion boards objectively base their selections on the performance demonstrated in the records of the officers they evaluate. Some white officers believed that affirmative action played a role in promotion outcomes, and that minorities and women were selected more often than their records warranted. White officers often mentioned shortcomings in education and experience as factors leading to lower promotion rates among black officers. Some also suggested that commissioning standards were lower for minorities than they were for whites. These perceptions caused many black officers to feel a disproportionate need to demonstrate their competency in each assignment. Our data did not record information about college preparation or other pre-commissioning background, so we could not address these perceptions in our quantitative analysis.

Discussions with both white and black male officers suggested that black officers have greater difficulties forming the peer and mentor relationships that many observers point to as being a key component of a successful career. While we could not objectively measure differences in the ability to form and draw from such relationships, both white and black participants made it clear that a certain level of social segregation continues to exist between the two groups. To avoid being seen as biased, many black officers hesitate to form the same close working relationships with other black officers that are common among white officers.

At the same time, participants from both groups noted that the services' assignment policies, which are perceived to disproportionately place black officers in ROTC and recruiting posts, serve to pull black males out of the usual assignments associated with their occupations. While these policies are intended to boost minority commission rates, such assignments are also thought by most to lower, not raise, officers' career trajectories.

Another hypothesis suggested to explain black-white career differences—that black officers are bid away by the private sector—was not borne out empirically. During the years that most officers leave of their own volition (before promotion to O-4), blacks are more likely, not less likely, to stay than were whites. Furthermore, survey data show almost no difference in perceived civilian job opportunities.

The interviews and focus groups revealed that women perceive limited occupational roles, concerns about harassment issues by both men and women, and competing family obligations to be the main reasons why female officers separate from the military at substantially greater rates than do men. As for black officers, these factors cause female officers to have greater difficulty forming effective peer and mentoring relationships and to hesitate to network with other women. Black female officers reported feeling that they were doubly disadvantaged, experiencing the problems of being both black and female.

Women officers continue to be concentrated in occupations perceived to offer more limited long-term career opportunities. Concentration of women in support occupations appears to have had little effect on career opportunities through the O-4 level, but female officers clearly believed that their traditional noncombat roles provided limited opportunities to advance to senior ranks, O-6 and above.

Women also suggested in the sessions that their role in the military is not fully accepted and that their physical and leadership abilities are often questioned. Men and women participants held substantial differences of opinion over whether it is appropriate for women to serve in any combat role, including those opened in recent years to women. Many men opposed combat roles for women. In contrast, most women wanted these opportunities available to qualified women, although some women preferred the opportunity to be voluntary. All the officers we talked to stressed the importance of maintaining high qualification and performance standards for officers, particularly those with combat responsibilities. However, opinions about the ability of women to meet these standards differed.

Many women also reported having experienced some form of harassment, often early in their careers. Both men and women indicated that to avoid any possibility of a harassment charge, many men avoid close working relationships with their female colleagues and subordinates. Regardless of gender, officers prefer to handle problems within the chain of command and tend to feel that the harassment training they had received was often ineffective.

Finally, women officers in our sample noted that they face considerably different and competing family obligations than do men. Married women officers are more likely to have an employed spouse and far more likely to have a military spouse, which makes it difficult to aggressively pursue a military career. Children make that situation even more difficult.

SUGGESTIONS FOR CHANGE

Officers in our interviews and focus groups pointed to several steps the Department of Defense (DoD) could take to improve the career progress of minority male and female officers:

- Recruit more women and minorities into the officer corps and into underrepresented occupations. Officers believed that many obstacles they have faced result from their standing out in units predominantly staffed with white males.

- Better inform all officers about career-management policies, especially those dealing with race and gender.

- Avoid atypical assignment policies wherever possible.

- Ensure that criteria for assigning individuals to occupations and assignments are appropriate and applied equally.

- Reevaluate the content and frequency of harassment training. If the real objective is to promote effective teamwork and constructive conflict resolution, reorientation of training content may be appropriate.

- Develop more effective mechanisms for handling harassment complaints within the chain of command.

- Encourage family-friendly practices.

- Promote acceptance of the role defined by policy for women in the military.

We are grateful for the support we received from a number of individuals in our sponsoring office. Keith Maxie initially managed the DoD study and actively supported our effort, providing guidance on focus and facilitating the visits we made to service headquarters offices and installations. We also valued highly the productive working relationship we had with Dr. Curtis Gilroy and Dr. John Enns in the later stages of the project. Frank Rush provided, as he always does, support and guidance throughout our effort. We also benefited from interactions with Dr. Steven Mehay, Dr. Mark Eitelberg, and their students at the Naval Postgraduate School, who conducted companion research. The Defense Manpower Data Center provided data files and, as always, answered our many questions about the data.

This project would not have been possible without the generous support of those responsible for officer management policy in each of the military services, who provided volumes of materials and answers to our many questions. We are equally indebted to the many officers who participated in focus groups and interviews; their thoughtful discussion of their own careers and their observation of fellow officers' careers form the backbone of our research. Organizing our visits required a considerable effort by the base personnel offices, and we would like to thank the personnel in these offices who bore the burden.

We would also like to thank our RAND colleagues who contributed in various ways to the project. Krista Perreira assisted with an analysis of the career progression of Army officers. Paul Koegel helped develop our interview protocols and participated in some of the interviews with headquarters staff and promotion board members. Mark Spranca helped the project team think through many difficult issues regarding race, prejudice, and discrimination. Early in the project, the military officers from all four services who were assigned as RAND fellows participated in discussions leading to the design of our focus groups. Laura Miller of the University of California at Los Angeles and Robert Schoeni made a number of valuable suggestions in their reviews of an earlier draft. Afshin Rastegar and Marian Oshiro prepared the data files we used in our analyses. Gordon Lee wrote the summary for this report and gave us good advice throughout the project on how to present our results. Irene Sanchez provided administrative support for the project and prepared the manuscript.

Chapter One

INTRODUCTION

With President Truman's 1948 executive order requiring "equality of treatment and opportunity for all persons in the armed services without regard to race, color, religion, or national origin," the military became a leader in the pursuit of equal opportunity for minorities, especially for African Americans.[1] Neither Title VII of the Civil Rights Act of 1964 nor the equal employment opportunity or affirmative action regulations of the Equal Employment Opportunity Commission apply to active-duty military officers. Instead, officers are covered by a Department of Defense (DoD) equal opportunity program based on a Human Goals Charter first issued by the Secretary of Defense in 1969. This charter establishes DoD's goal to "provide everyone in the military the opportunity to rise to as high a level of responsibility as possible, based only on individual talent and diligence."[2]

This goal of equal opportunity now applies to women as well as minorities except as the service of women is constrained by law and policy. The law has changed over time; currently, there are no longer statutory restrictions. By policy women are restricted from serving in occupations or units whose mission is to engage in direct ground combat. Congressional consultation would be required to lift this policy.

---

[1]Throughout this report, we use the terms African American and black interchangeably.

[2]This information is taken from U.S. General Accounting Office (GAO), November 1995.

In a 1994 memorandum, Secretary of Defense William Perry reaffirmed DoD's commitment to equal opportunity and asked the Under Secretary of Defense for Personnel and Readiness to conduct a "study of the officer 'pipeline,' and where necessary, to recommend ways to improve the flow of minority and female officers from recruitment through general and flag officer ranks." The research documented in this report was undertaken in support of this officer pipeline study (Gilroy et al., 1999).

MOTIVATION AND CONTEXT FOR THE OFFICER PIPELINE STUDY

To motivate his equal opportunity directives, Secretary Perry referred to the military's proud history as a leader "in expanding opportunities for minority groups," to DoD employees' right to "carry out their jobs without discrimination or harassment," and to the "military and economic necessity" of equal opportunity.

The memorandum was written at a time when equal opportunity and harassment were issues of general public concern and changing legal status. Some similar issues had appeared in the military in the 1990s. For example, several highly publicized incidents of harassment of women service members had occurred, notably at the Tailhook Convention in 1991.

More generally, data showed patterns of decreasing diversity with rank. In 1994, a higher percentage of junior officers than senior officers were women or minorities (Figure 1).[3] In contrast, the enlisted force included more minorities than either officer group at all levels of seniority and showed no diversity differences between the junior and senior ranks. As a result there were potentially undesirable differences in racial and ethnic diversity between the "rank and file" and their leadership. On the other hand, women made up the same fraction of the enlisted and officer groups at junior and senior ranks.

---

[3]This pattern has not changed in the past few years. (Office of the Assistant Secretary of Defense, 1998)

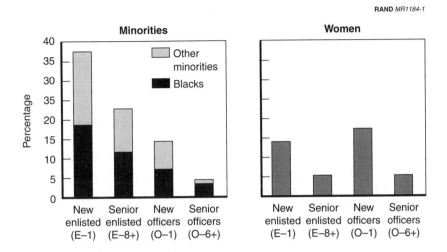

Figure 1—Race and Ethnicity of Military Personnel, 1994

At first glance, these patterns of declining diversity at more senior ranks are not surprising. There are bound to be relatively few minority and female senior officers because minorities accounted for under 4 percent of the officers commissioned 25 to 30 years ago, when today's senior officers entered service, and women accounted for no more than 2 percent of new officers in those years. Based on these numbers, we can infer that much of the difference between the junior and senior officer ranks in 1994 was probably historical. However, we cannot rule out the possibility that some of the diversity gap resulted from lower rates of career progression for minority and women officers who entered service at various points in time. To disentangle the effects of increasing diversity at entry with the effects of any subsequent differences in career progression, one must track groups of entering officers over time and measure the promotion and retention rates for different racial, ethnic, and gender groups.

A November 1995 General Accounting Office (GAO) report included a more direct analysis of racial and gender disparities in accessions, assignments, and promotions. The report found some disparities, with the most common ones for officers occurring in promotions. However, as the GAO report noted, their analysis was relatively straightforward, and more detailed and comprehensive information is needed to determine whether DoD's equal opportunity goal is being met. The purpose of this project is to add information and understanding.

GENERAL STUDY DESIGN

The project examined the career progression of minority and female officers, compared with white male officers, through two strands of research. The first strand analyzed officer personnel records to determine whether minority and female officers had been promoted and retained at the same rates as white male officers. The second strand consisted of interviews with individuals who manage officers and select them for promotion, and both interviews and focus groups involving middle-ranking officers (primarily grades O-3 and O-4). The interviews with the officer management staff in each service focused on the policies and procedures that direct officer careers. Our purpose in talking to members of promotion boards was to understand the board process and identify key factors leading to promotion for all officers. The interviews and focus groups with midcareer officers explored how officers generally progress in their careers and real or perceived differences in the experiences of minority and female officers. Most of the minority officers in the interviews and focus groups were black, but some Hispanic officers participated as well.

The data analysis evaluated the personnel records of officers from seven commissioning cohorts: 1967, 1970, 1977, 1980, 1983, 1987, and 1991.[4] We tracked the members of each cohort until they left service or through 1994. We interviewed personnel managers and policy implementers at each service's headquarters and personnel center. We visited four bases, one from each service, to talk to a cross-section of officers in the middle ranks. These discussions, which were conducted in mid-1995, were carried out through one-on-one interviews and in focus groups organized by race and gender.

------

[4]This data file was originally constructed for the Naval Postgraduate School. It included data for the 1997 cohort, but we dropped this cohort from our analysis because it had extensive data errors that could not be easily corrected.

We talked to white male officers as well as minority and female officers.

In fiscal year (FY) 1995, the racial/ethnic composition of officers in the middle ranks were (across all services): 86 percent white, 8 percent black, 3 percent Hispanic, and 3 percent other racial/ethnic groups.[5] Hispanics are a diverse group, with many socioeconomic and cultural differences between the subgroups (e.g., Cuban Americans, Mexican Americans). The final group, which we call "other," is similarly diverse. Our data analysis considered all of these groups. However, we largely limited the interviews and focus groups to white and black officers (male and female) because it was not possible within this project's scope to adequately explore career issues with the other racial/ethnic groups. Other research has found that military career experiences differ for blacks and other minorities.

Both study components only considered officers not belonging to professional occupations. Officers in the professions—e.g., physicians, nurses, dentists, chaplains, and lawyers—are managed separately in all services except the Marine Corps and often have atypical career patterns. This restriction to line officers most affected our analysis of female officers because one-half of them are in professional occupations, primarily in health. In contrast, just over one-fifth of both white and black officers are in these occupations.

ORGANIZATION OF THE REPORT

The next chapter provides an overview of officer careers, the performance evaluation and promotion selection processes in each service, and specific policies or practices affecting minorities and women. Chapter Three describes our analysis of officer personnel records and Chapters Four and Five summarize the results of our interviews and focus groups with midcareer officers. Both chapters include a summary of the analytic methods used, but they focus on the results. Additional technical details are included in the appendices to the re-

---

[5]These data are from the Office of the Assistant Secretary of Defense (Force Management Policy), 1996, and are for officers in the O-3 and O-4 pay grades (see Chapter Two for an explanation of pay grades). The data for FY 1997 are similar; whites decreased to 85 percent and other minorities increased to 4 percent.

port. The final chapter integrates the findings from the two analyses in an overall assessment of the career progression of black and female officers.

DESCRIPTION OF AN OFFICER'S CAREER

COMMISSION SOURCES

Most officers receive their commission through one of three sources: the service academies, Reserve Officer Training Corps (ROTC) programs at public and private civilian institutions, or Officer Candidate or Training School[1] (OCS/OTS). All four services also have programs to allow promising young enlisted personnel to complete their college degree and earn a commission. The applicants, benefits, academic and military preparation, active-duty service obligation, and career-field opportunities differ for each of the three sources (academy, ROTC, and OCS/OTS). Most new officers are entering military service for the first time, but some have prior enlisted service.

Until recently, entering officers were given either a "regular" or "reserve" commission, depending on their commissioning source and undergraduate record.[2] In the Army, Navy, and Air Force, augmentation from a reserve to a regular commission is automatic at some point with the tender of a regular commission upon selection for promotion. However, when this research was conducted, the Marine Corps selected for augmentation in separate boards that op-

---

[1]The Air Force program is called Officer Training School.

[2]An active-duty officer with a reserve commission is different from an officer in one of the reserve components. The 1992 National Defense Authorization Act mandated that *all* officers commissioned after September 1996 must enter active duty with a "reserve" commission and then pass through the augmentation process before receiving admission to the "regular" officer corps.

erated like promotion boards.[3] The number of officers who may be augmented varies substantially from year to year and across career fields.

Service Academies

The three service academies[4] provide officer candidates with a rigorous academic program and a complete immersion into military life. Admission to the academies is highly competitive, requiring very high academic, physical, and social accomplishment. Academy cadets receive free tuition, other expenses, and a stipend ($600/ month). In return, academy graduates generally incur a basic active-duty service obligation of five years.

Academy graduates begin their careers with a number of advantages. By the time that academy graduates begin their active duty, they are well steeped in the procedures and expectations of their service. They enter with a sizable cohort of peers with whom they have formed friendships and working relationships. They also receive regular commissions, and they are more likely to be placed in the occupation they prefer.

ROTC Programs

ROTC officer candidates pursue a bachelor's degree program at a civilian college or university while receiving credits toward their degree from a sequence of ROTC military education classes. There are a number of regular and scholarship ROTC arrangements. Regular candidates receive only a small stipend ($150/month) during their junior and senior years and incur a correspondingly modest two- to three-year active-duty obligation. Select ROTC officer candidates receive scholarships that cover part or all of their tuition and other expenses and provide a $1,500/year stipend. They must spend four years on active duty.

---

[3]More recently, the Marine Corps ended this practice and combined augmentation with promotion selection.

[4]The Naval Academy educates officer candidates for both the Navy and Marine Corps, which does not maintain its own academy.

More than 600 public and private universities and colleges have ROTC programs. The academic quality of these schools ranges from the most highly selective to relatively less selective. Officers we interviewed reported that the quality of military education also varies substantially between ROTC programs, although there was no consensus about which types of colleges were likely to have better programs. Thus, in contrast to academy graduates, the academic and military preparation of officers commissioned through ROTC programs is likely to vary more substantially.

OCS/OTS Programs

As in ROTC programs, OCS/OTS officer candidates receive their bachelor's degree from civilian institutions. However, most have no military education as college students. OCS/OTS officer candidates go through an intense 10- to 16-week program centered on basic military education, and they incur a four-year active-duty obligation. Depending on the requirements in different career fields at the time they are commissioned, officers with commissions through OCS/OTS often have a more limited choice of career field and initial duty assignment than do officers from other programs. Until recently, they also entered with a reserve commission—at the time, a disadvantage mostly in the Marine Corps.

In the Marine Corps, OCS is the final precommissioning activity for a unique program called the Platoon Leaders Course (PLC). PLC in some ways resembles ROTC because candidates sign up while they are students in a civilian college. However, they do not attend classes during the school year—only during a special summer program—and they do not oblige themselves to serve until they graduate. As we will show in Chapter Three, PLC is by far the largest commissioning source for Marine officers.

Enlisted Commissioning Programs

The services have a number of programs that provide young enlisted personnel with opportunities to receive an officer commission. These programs often cover the cost to complete a bachelor's degree, usually at a civilian institution but occasionally at a service academy.

Candidates who attend a civilian institution must also complete either a ROTC or an OCS/OTS program. Enlisted personnel apply to these programs and their applications are considered by formal selection boards.

Many of the officers we talked to said that individuals with prior enlisted service are generally quite successful as junior officers. These officers already have become acculturated to military life and acquired military skills, allowing them to focus their attention on learning the occupation they enter as an officer. However, these officers reach basic retirement eligibility (at 20 years of service) earlier than their peers due to their prior enlisted time. As a result, considerably fewer prior service officers remain in service beyond O-4 (see Chapter Three).

Accession of Minorities and Women

There are numerous reasons why a diverse officer corps is thought to be desirable. For example, equal opportunity to serve as an officer is integral to the military's overall commitment to equal opportunity. It is considered desirable to have officers who generally resemble the enlisted personnel they lead. In addition, officers are visible representatives of the American people when they are deployed overseas.

In a general way, all the services seek diversity, but there were few specific goals at the time of this study. Only the Marine Corps, which has by far the fewest women, had specific plans to increase the number of female officers. The objective was to move from less than 4 percent of all officers in 1995 to more than 7 percent by 2004–2010. Only the Navy and Marine Corps had explicit goals for the level of representation of minorities. In 1994, Secretary of the Navy Dalton established a plan for increasing minority accessions to 10–12 percent African American, 10–12 percent Hispanic, and 4–5 percent Asian-Pacific Islander by the year 2000. The 12-12-5 goals were derived from the representation of these minority groups in the U.S. population, rather than in the enlisted ranks or college-graduate population.

The services have a number of programs that target minority officer recruiting.[5] The first of these focuses on ROTC units at Historically Black Colleges and Universities (HBCUs). HBCUs account for a significant proportion of black officer accessions in all the services; in 1996, 43 percent of black accessions were from HBCUs. The Army has several programs that target HBCUs. The Quality Enrichment Program awards ROTC scholarships at HBCUs; because of this program, Moskos and Butler reported in 1996 that a black scholarship applicant is twice as likely to receive a scholarship as a white applicant is. Similarly, the most generous scholarships for enlisted personnel—which are for four years—are offered only at these schools. Since 1995, the Navy and Marine Corps' Immediate and Express Scholarship Decision Programs have awarded scholarships to well-qualified high school students; although not a targeted program, the awards have included high fractions of blacks and Hispanics (one-fifth) and women (one-third). All three services operate preparatory schools to help selected academy applicants qualify for admission. In recent years, the preparatory schools have provided 30 percent or more of the minority students at the academies. Finally, since minorities have a higher representation in the enlisted ranks than they do in the officer corps, the various enlisted commissioning programs described above are an important source of minority officers. To encourage participation in these programs, the services have assigned minority officers to targeted recruiting duty.

INITIAL OFFICER LISTING

In all services but the Air Force, the individual officers in a cohort are ordered in an "order of merit" list at or just after the time they enter active duty. The other services consider this initial listing in determining officers' career branches or fields, their initial assignments, and timing of subsequent promotion. An officer's placement on the list for his/her cohort is based on his or her date of commission. Officers commissioned on the same date are ordered according to their academic grades, military education grades, and performance during military field exercises; the specific weights given to each

---

[5]For more information on the Army's targeted accession programs and other programs aimed at minorities, see Moskos and Butler (1996). Information on these and other programs is also included in the DoD Pipeline Report.

component vary somewhat from service to service. Academy graduates are always the first to receive commissions in a particular entry cohort; thus, by definition, their initial listings are always higher than are those of regular ROTC officer candidates.[6]

In contrast to the other services, the Marine Corps does not determine its initial officer listing until the end of The (Officer) Basic School (TBS). As in the Army and Navy, the Marine Corps uses a composite score of academic grades, military education grades, and leadership evaluations based on field exercise performance. However, the grades are derived solely from performance and testing during TBS; academic or military education grades prior to TBS and one's source of commission do not directly affect a candidate's listing.

CAREER FIELD SELECTION AND DUTY ASSIGNMENT

A young officer's career potential is influenced by his or her career field and duty assignments. Ideally, the career field is a good match for the individual's abilities and preferences, allows the young officer to demonstrate performance in responsible positions, and has a relatively large number of senior positions. Similarly, an ambitious officer wants to be assigned to key positions within his or her career field. Good occupational and duty assignments are those that provide the opportunity for an officer to demonstrate the superior performance needed for promotion to senior ranks.

Career Field (Occupation) Assignment

The assignment of career field is handled slightly differently, depending on an officer's accession source and service. The most common procedure is for officer candidates to submit "dream sheets" listing several choices for career field placement. Marine Corps officers submit their dream sheets near the end of TBS. In all other services, officer candidates submit their dream sheets near the end of their respective accession program (academy, ROTC, or OCS/OTS).

---

[6]ROTC scholarship and distinguished military graduates from regular ROTC programs are often ranked with academy graduates in the Lineal List/Order of Merit List.

The services assign career fields based on their needs and the individuals' academic and physical qualifications and occupational preferences, giving priority to the former. Certain technical fields also require a special qualification test; otherwise, the assignment is made based on the general and specific skills of the officer. By law, women cannot serve in ground combat occupations or assignments; before 1993–94, women were excluded from other occupations and assignments that carried a risk of exposure to combat (Harrell and Miller, 1997). To ensure quality personnel in all career fields, the Marine Corps has instituted a rule of thirds: one-third of the placements in a career field must come from each of the top, middle, and bottom third of the Order of Merit ranking.

The selection of pilots in all services tends to be a notable exception to these general procedures. Marine Corps officer candidates who wish to serve as pilots usually prearrange this placement before entering TBS.[7] Most Marine Corps pilots receive commissions through the Naval Academy or ROTC. In the Air Force, it used to be common for nearly all academy graduates to receive placements as pilot trainees, if they qualified physically. However, the force drawdown has cut the available pilot training seats in half and has caused an increasing proportion of Air Force Academy graduates to be placed in other career fields.

Similar to the selection of career field, initial base or ship assignment is determined by the needs of the service, the preferences of the officer, and the officer's initial ranking or performance in training. Within a career field, the first assignments differ primarily in their location. For example, the standard first assignment for infantry officers in the Army and Marine Corps is as a platoon leader. The processes by which subsequent assignments are determined vary quite a bit from service to service.

Duty Assignment

In the Army and the Marine Corps, officers work with their assignment officers to arrange their future assignments. Usually, each as-

---

[7] Each TBS company can designate a small number of qualified officers for aviation occupations.

signment officer manages all officers of a given rank in a particular community or occupational specialty. The assignment officer is given the list of available positions and works with officers under his or her management to appropriately match individuals to positions.

An assignment officer's primary responsibility is to meet the needs of the service; the needs and preferences of the individual are of secondary importance. While it is generally in the interest of the service to ensure that all officers be given appropriate opportunities to develop their career, the short-term needs of the services may at times run counter to this. Thus, individuals must be proactive in managing their career after the first assignment. Individuals must sometimes be explicit in requesting career-enhancing assignments, as an assignment officer cannot always present individuals with the best opportunities. The services have developed career-information guides that describe key assignments and other requirements for promotion.

Army and Marine Corps officers can sometimes prearrange good assignments. An office with an open billet can request that the assignment officer fill the position with a particular officer. Depending on the office making the request and the career development of the officer of whom the request is made, the assignment officer may or may not choose to honor the request. Army and Marine Corps assignment officers reported that such requests are more common for high-visibility positions such as Pentagon or headquarters assignments.

The Navy assignment system is similar to the Army and Marine Corps system except that it involves both an assignment officer, called a detailer, and a placement officer. The detailer manages officer assignments and is responsible for balancing the officer's career needs with the needs of the Navy. The placement officer serves as a particular command's point of contact in the assignment process. Placement officers are responsible for balancing the needs of a command with the needs of the officers assigned to fill the billets.

Although the responsibility for career counseling in the Navy rests with the officer's commanding officer, detailers are expected to keep an eye on the career progress of officers assigned to them, and to help officers identify career-enhancing moves. The detailer also must "sell" some officers on duty assignments that may be less career-enhancing. As with Army and Marine Corps assignment officers, Navy detailers are judged primarily by their ability to fill billets based on the needs of the Navy. As in the Army and Marine Corps, Navy personnel reported that officers can sometimes prearrange desirable assignments.

The Air Force's assignment system closely resembled that of the other services until 1991, when it was replaced by a voluntary assignment system supported by an electronic bulletin board listing job openings. The bulletin board lists all openings for line officers below O-6, except for some key positions—e.g., commanders (squadron and above) and generals' personal staffs. Officers are supposed to start reviewing the listings in their career field many months before their current assignment ends and apply for the positions they find most interesting. If they don't find a position by the time they must be reassigned, their assignment officer matches them to a job in the traditional manner.[8] In our interviews and focus groups, Air Force officers consistently reported that few jobs advertised on the bulletin board were filled by an applicant from the bulletin board. However, the bulletin board does provide information about the kinds of jobs available, which can be useful in working with an assignment officer.

Occupation and Assignment for Minorities and Women

All career fields and assignments have been open to blacks and other minorities for many years. However, minority officers continue to be overrepresented in occupations such as supply and underrepresented in the tactical occupations. In the Navy, minority officers are overrepresented in the surface community and underrepresented in the submarine community (see Chapter Three).

Unlike male minorities, women are excluded from certain occupations and assignments. These restrictions, which have eased over

---

[8]When first implemented, officers could not be assigned to a job for which they did not volunteer. The voluntary system was recently modified to allow for nonvoluntary assignment of officers who don't have a voluntary assignment when they come up for mandatory reassignment. This change was made to allow the Air Force to fill important but undesirable positions.

time and have been reduced significantly since 1993, are described in some detail in Harrell and Miller (1997). Since a series of policy changes in 1993–94, women have been restricted from serving only in occupations or assignments that directly engage in ground combat. Harrell and Miller report that the percentage of all officer and enlisted positions closed to women decreased from 33 to 20 between 1993 and 1997. This figure is now lower than 1 percent in the Air Force, 9 percent in the Navy, and about 30 percent in the Army and Marine Corps. It is important to note that women may now perform many of the key jobs in the Air Force and Navy—including flying combat aircraft and serving on all but the smallest combat surface ships. The ground combat exclusion policy keeps women out of many combat jobs in the other two services. Despite the changes in opportunities for women, most remain in traditionally female occupations such as personnel and administration (see Chapter Three).

The Army and Marine Corps require new male officers to include at least one combat occupation in the choices they list on an occupational dream sheet. This requirement and the Marine Corps' rule of thirds, described above, help to limit the disproportionate assignment of any minority group to any occupation. The Army convenes a selection board to assign ROTC graduates to occupational branches; the usual equal opportunity goals, described below, apply to these boards as they do to all formal selection boards. During our interviews, we were told about less formal initiatives to encourage more blacks to enter combat career fields. For example, there are efforts to provide more information about the career fields to new officers and invite them to meet with minority role models from these occupations.

There are also some formal procedures for assuring fairness in duty assignments after the officer has been assigned to an occupation. The Navy now reviews all minority assignments with a goal of eliminating disparities in nonminority and minority assignments. Increasingly, all the services are using formal selection boards for key assignments, such as command assignments; as indicated above, these boards are guided by precepts that set fairness goals for minorities and women.

The services have, at times, consciously filled certain assignments in recruiting, ROTC instruction, and equal opportunity with women and minorities. This has been done in the belief that the presence of women and minorities as visible role models in such positions enhances the accession and retention of other minority or female officers. Yet this practice can also lead some officers to consider such assignments as "minority" or "female" assignments, a perspective that can devalue strong performance in such assignments. It can also hinder the ability of minorities and women to develop valuable experience and competitive career records if it limits their time in critical jobs within their occupations. Finally, the practice potentially limits the number of minority and female officers available to serve as peers, mentors, and role models for other more junior officers in operational units, where peer support and mentoring may be most valuable.

PERFORMANCE EVALUATIONS

In all four services, an officer receives written performance evaluations. A description of the format used by each service may be found in Appendix A. These evaluations constitute the primary record of an officer's performance and are reviewed by selection boards (for augmentation, advanced education, promotion, and command) and those who make duty assignment selections. Generally, the evaluations are written by each officer's immediate supervisor and reviewed by a more senior rater. Although the specific format varies by service and has varied within the services over time, there are some common elements. The evaluation consists of brief written descriptions of the officer's job; his/her notable accomplishments during the period being evaluated (usually a year); his/her overall performance and potential; and recommendations for next career steps. In addition to the written comments, the officer's performance is rated on one or more scales.

As officers progress through the ranks, their evaluations are given more or less weight depending on the job in which the officer is being rated and the identity of the senior rater. The more challenging the job, the more weight the performance evaluation carries; the same may be true for performance evaluations written by high-ranking officers.

If an officer feels he or she has received an unfair or discriminatory performance evaluation, there is a formal appeals process. If the appeal is successful, the evaluation form is removed from the officer's personnel record and a notice of the removal is included. Officers may write a letter to the promotion board that clarifies their record.

Inflation in Performance Evaluation

In a competitive environment, performance evaluations often become inflated. Inflation over time has long been universal across the services and common to performance evaluation systems in the private sector as well. With inflated grading, the language used to describe the officer and his/her performance takes on paramount importance; an example is the difference between an "excellent" officer (not quite up to snuff), an "outstanding" officer (a good officer), and the "best officer in his/her year group" (an outstanding officer).

According to the officer managers we interviewed, the competitive assignment and promotion system and the inflation in performance evaluations have led to a widespread perception that a "zero-defect" career is needed to be successful. Performance that is reported as being less than outstanding is seen to doom a career, even at lower ranks when officers are learning and might be expected to have room for performance improvement. Officers who make mistakes or run into serious problems may feel they have little opportunity to learn from their mistakes in such a system. Though detailers and selection board members are quite adept at interpreting the performance evaluation "code" in inflated evaluations, from time to time the services find it necessary to "reset the system" by introducing a new performance evaluation tool.[9]

We were also told that young officers often take some time to correctly interpret performance evaluations. An "excellent" officer who has received two or three Bs among the A grades may not realize that his or her performance is actually being rated below average. As officers gain more experience in reading and interpreting performance evaluations, it is not unusual for them to provide input to their performance evaluation. This input may range from a list of job accomplishments all the way to a complete draft of the performance evaluation.

---

[9]The Army phased in a new evaluation form in FY 1998.

PROMOTION

Officers advance by being promoted to a sequence of "pay grades." The rank titles that are associated with each pay grade differ across the services (see Table 1), but the level of responsibility and authority accompanying each grade is roughly standard. The Defense Officer Personnel Management Act of 1980 (DOPMA) standardized much of the management of officer careers across the four services.[10] In particular, DOPMA set common targets for grade-to-grade promotion rates. The "up or out" system requires most officers to separate from active duty if they fail to make promotion to the next grade within a fixed period of time.

If the officer completes training, promotion from O-1 to O-2 is essentially automatic, and voluntary separations are not likely as most service obligations last four years or longer. Over the past 15 years, the services have lost on average only about 5 percent of a commission cohort before the members reached O-2. "Wash-outs" from basic military or occupational training are the major source of separations during the first couple of years. The physical and intellectual standards a young officer must meet differ somewhat according to occupational field; for example, combat arms specialists must meet especially challenging leadership and physical standards, while nuclear specialists must pass a series of difficult academic tests.

Table 1

Officer Pay Grades and Associated Rank Titles

Grade	Army, Air Force, and Marine Corps	Navy
O-1	Second Lieutenant	Ensign
O-2	First Lieutenant	Lieutenant Junior Grade
O-3	Captain	Lieutenant
O-4	Major	Lieutenant Commander
O-5	Lieutenant Colonel	Commander
O-6	Colonel	Captain
O-7 to O-10	General officers	Flag officers

---

[10]See Rostker et al., 1993.

Survival to O-4 is determined primarily by two factors: an individual's choice to continue his or her military service and demonstration of the level of performance needed for promotion to the first "field grade" of O-4. Somewhat more officers leave voluntarily than fail to receive the O-3 or O-4 promotion (see Chapter Three). Officers generally complete their initial service obligation while at the O-3 level, and about one-third choose to end their service at that time.

In contrast to the O-2 promotion, the O-3 and O-4 promotions are considered "competitive" in that candidates undergo a competitive board review process. However, since DOPMA sets the O-3 promotion rate goal at 95 percent (Table 2), the O-3 promotion at about four years is also virtually automatic. The O-4 promotion, occurring around ten years, is the first truly competitive promotion. About one-fifth of the officers reviewed by the O-4 promotion board will not be selected and will subsequently be required to separate from the services. Although some of these nonselected officers may be allowed to continue in service for a while, they will generally not be able to reach retirement unless they have prior enlisted service.

Attaining senior ranks requires the demonstration of a sustained manner of excellence in performance. To be competitive for promotion to O-5 and above, officers must begin building the necessary credentials early in their career. The promotion board members we interviewed said that "slow starts" must be over before an officer attains O-3. Further, officers must ensure that they demonstrate performance in difficult or key assignments in their career field. Selection for and good performance in the most challenging and

Table 2

DOPMA Model of Officer Careers

Grade	Promotion Opportunity (% promoted)	Promotion Timing (YOS)	Cumulative Probability to Grade from Original Cohort (includes expected attrition)
O-2	100% if fully qualified	2.0	96%
O-3	95%	3.5/4	82%
O-4	80%	10±1	66%
O-5	70%	16±1	41%
O-6	50%	22±1	18%

SOURCE: Rostker et al. (1993), p. 14.
NOTE: YOS = Years of service.

prestigious assignments are marks of success. Opportunities in non-combat-related career fields often peak in the later career stage as the relative number of general officer positions in these fields is rather limited. Senior billets are particularly limited for officers in the administrative and personnel career fields.

In addition to demonstrating sustained excellence in performance, officers must acquire certain credentials to be considered competitive for promotion to senior ranks. One important credential is the completion of required professional military educational (PME) courses or other expected civilian advanced degree programs. Officers can complete PME courses either by correspondence or in residence. Since selection to attend the more advanced PME courses in residence is competitive, this is often a signal of prior high performance. In order to be competitive for promotion to senior ranks in the Air Force, officers also are expected to complete a postgraduate civilian program. Completion of the expected educational programs is not always a technical requirement for promotion but is generally seen as a "de facto" standard.

The Promotion Selection Process

Generally, all officers in a cohort are considered for each new promotion at the same time; the legislated schedule was shown earlier in Table 2, but the actual promotions to grades O-4 and beyond have tended to occur about two years later. The exceptions are officers who earlier in their careers were selected for an early or late promotion; they then join the cohort one or more years ahead or behind. When evaluated, officers may be below the "zone" (the primary year of eligibility for the promotion), in the zone, and above the zone. The fractions selected from below the zone and above the zone vary across services and cohorts, but typically about 90 percent are chosen when first eligible in the zone.

The substance of the deliberation is essentially the same in all services, although the process by which promotion selection boards deliberate differs. Promotion board deliberations are based on the contents of the candidate's file, which includes a cover sheet that details the officer's assignment history, military and civilian educational certifications, distinctions and honors, performance evaluations, and any reports of judicial punishments or admonishments.

Navy, Army, and Marine Corps files also include photographs, which are used to evaluate military bearing (e.g., posture, grooming, and fitness).

Basic credentials for promotion include: completion of appropriate military education courses and/or relevant civilian postgraduate degrees, qualification in their military occupations, a record of performance and good conduct, and (in the Marine Corps at this time) augmentation to a regular commission.[11]

Beyond these basic credentials, candidates must demonstrate to board members a sustained level of performance and a potential for future leadership. Board members assess these qualities primarily through a review of the candidate's assignment history and performance evaluations. The performance threshold increases as the promotions become more competitive.

Board members look for a sequence of assignments appropriate for the career field and particularly difficult, critical, or high-profile assignments. These include the assignments listed in the career guides we alluded to earlier. Individuals with atypical assignment histories can have difficulty demonstrating career-field credibility. Atypical histories develop for a variety of reasons—for example, switching career fields several years into one's career, accepting an otherwise atypical position in order to co-locate with a spouse, or failing to get important assignments due to past poor performance.[12] Board members are instructed to leave room in their evaluations for "slow starts" and "nontraditional" career paths. However, in choosing among officers who are borderline, board members often must consider all career irregularities, even those that occurred early in a career. A single negative evaluation can be overcome, but only if it is followed by a higher manner of performance.

---

[11]Before augmentation was tied to promotion selection, Marine officers could apply for augmentation any time after their second year and after receiving at least one fitness report in an operational assignment. Given the year-to-year variation in available regular commission slots, it was important that an officer apply early and often for augmentation, but not all officers did so.

[12]Important assignments typically include responsible positions on the command staff for a high-level unit (e.g., battalion), as a department head on a Navy ship, or as a unit commander.

Good performance is indicated by being ranked high in a group of peers or receiving the highest absolute scores. The wording of reviews by senior raters is particularly important, especially if the wording demonstrates a familiarity with and sincerity in the review of a candidate. Officers demonstrate potential for leadership through strong performance in command positions and through the explicit enthusiastic recommendations by senior raters for future command assignments or for selection for in-residence professional military education.

Boards follow a formal process to ensure fairness. Prior to deliberating, boards are provided precepts, signed by the service Secretary. The precepts specify the number of officers who can be promoted and set goals for officers in certain career fields and with joint duty assignments. The precepts also set equal opportunity goals, which are further described below.[13] These are goals, not quotas.

All services have instituted procedures that can inform a board president throughout the proceeding on how well its results compare with the goals. Usually, the use of these procedures is at the discretion of the board president. The Army and the Air Force also track the voting patterns of individual board members to ensure that their voting shows no anomalous patterns, such as preferences for officers in a particular occupation, from any racial/ethnic group, or with any other characteristics not appropriately considered for promotion. Inappropriate use of the scoring scales are also identified (e.g., too many top scores).

Guidelines for Minorities and Women

The portions of the instructions to promotion boards (and other selection boards) that concern minorities and women, as they appeared at the time of our research, are reproduced in Appendix B. The Secretary of each service prepares these instructions in accordance with DoD Directive 1320.12, which requires that they include "guidelines to ensure the board considers all eligible officers without prejudice or partiality." The common Navy and Marine Corps in-

---

[13]Chapters Four and Five summarize what we learned about the implementation of these goals in our interviews and focus groups.

struction cited unspecified studies in urging board members not to overlook those minority officers (especially African Americans) who are "late bloomers" because of their past inexperience with a majority environment. All the instructions included two generally worded provisions: (1) Board members should be sensitive to the possibility of past discrimination and the reality of atypical assignment patterns; and (2) The board should review its selection rates for minorities and women and compare them with the selection rates for all officers. All the services except for the Air Force set a clear goal of equal selection rates. Finally, candidate files in all four services explicitly indicated an officer's race and gender.

Chapter Three

DIFFERENCES IN RETENTION AND PROMOTION FOR MINORITY AND FEMALE LINE OFFICERS

The purpose of our empirical analysis was to assess whether there are differences in career progression between officers in different racial, ethnic, and gender groups. Specifically, we wanted to compare:

- how officers in different minority/gender groups enter military service,

- whether they choose to stay in service, and

- whether they are selected for promotion.

These three career outcomes mix choices made by the officer and choices made by the officer's service. Before they are commissioned, officer candidates choose among the entry programs (commissioning sources) for which they qualify. Retention is a voluntary decision, although it is important to note that some individuals leave in anticipation of promotion failure and subsequent involuntary separation. On the other hand, promotion is an involuntary outcome from the officer's perspective. A particular goal of our analysis was to separate the voluntary outcome—retention—from the involuntary outcome—promotion.

THE OFFICER COHORT DATA FILES

To carry out this analysis, we used a specially created data file prepared by the Defense Manpower Data Center (DMDC); this file was originally prepared for researchers at the Naval Postgraduate School. The file included an extract of the Officer Master Record created at the end of each fiscal year served by every officer in seven cohorts: 1967, 1970, 1977, 1980, 1983, 1987, and 1991.[1] We also received first-year records for the 1994 cohort, which we used to compare entering characteristics over time. This chapter begins with a brief description of these data, followed by descriptions of changes in the minority and gender composition of the entering cohorts, the commissioning sources through which the officers prepared for military service, and the military occupations they entered. This chapter concludes with an analysis of the career progression of the different racial and gender officer groups in these cohorts.

The DMDC was only able to provide records beginning in 1977 for those officers still in service from the two earliest cohorts in our data file—1967 and 1970. For all cohorts, the last annual record was for 1993. Consistent with our focus, we deleted the records for officers in professional occupations (principally medical, legal, and religious professionals). Substantial proportions of women officers are represented in these fields, particularly the medical professions. Thus, the restriction eliminated slightly more than half of women officers from our study, but only one-fifth of the men. The restriction eliminated roughly the same proportion of whites, blacks, and other minorities from the study.[2]

These data provide limited information. For each person, the records indicate:

- Entry path: commissioning source, prior federal military service (used to determine prior service entrants), and military occupation;

---

[1]The cohorts are separated by three- or four-year intervals. In keeping with this pattern, the original data files included the 1973 cohort. However, the data for this cohort turned out to be unusable.

[2]In the 1977 cohort, 24 percent of male officers and 52 percent of female officers were in the professional occupations. By the 1991 cohort, 20 percent of male officers and 56 percent of female officers were in the professional occupations. In the 1977 cohort, 28 percent of white officers, 21 percent of black officers, and 50 percent of other minority officers were in the professional occupations. By the 1991 cohort, 27 percent of white officers, 26 percent of black officers, and 27 percent of other minority officers were in the professional occupations.

- Retention: inferred from the number of annual records;

- Promotion: inferred from pay grade in each year of active commissioned service;

- Personal characteristics: marital status and number of dependents (in each year), race/ethnicity, gender.

Defining Race and Ethnicity

Our preliminary analysis of these data uncovered inconsistencies in the recording of race and ethnicity across cohorts. Race and ethnicity were recorded in a single data element with a limited number of categories before 1980, but the records were revised to separate race and ethnicity after this date. In exploring these data to determine how best to handle this change, we discovered a pattern of changing racial and ethnic identification for Hispanic and Native American service members. In the later cohorts we studied, more members identified themselves as belonging to these ethnic groups, and more self-identified Hispanics and Native Americans listed their race as "other."[3] Similarly, some Hispanics and Native Americans in the earlier cohorts changed their racial designation over time.

To carry out this analysis of career progression, we needed to define racial and ethnic groups in a way that remained consistent over time. The most consistent classification possible over the long period of time covered by our data defines only three racial groups: white, black, and other. With this classification, some of the growth in the "other" group over time is misleading because it merely reflects the increasing tendency for Hispanics to list their race as other; the impact is negligible on the white group and virtually nonexistent for the black group.

_____

[3]See Appendix C for additional details on racial and ethnic identification in the military. Similar patterns are emerging in other data systems as well, including the U.S. Census, and they are described in three volumes: (1) National Research Council (1995); (2) Bean and Tienda (1987); and (3) Kissam et al. (1993).

DIVERSITY OF OFFICER ACCESSIONS OVER TIME

Table 3 shows how the racial and gender mix of officer accessions changed in the 1977–1991 cohorts, the years for which we have data.[4] Like all the data reported in this chapter, the table excludes officers in the scientific, legal, religious, and medical professions. After 1977, there was little change in diversity in the accession cohorts. There was an increase in the fraction of officers from other minority groups in the 1987 and 1991 cohorts. Some of this increase is illusory since it reflects the change in racial identification of Hispanics; unfortunately, no data exist that would allow us to quantify these changes in self-identification in the military. The fraction who were female increased from 9 percent in 1977 to 11 percent in 1991; since this figure varied over the time period, there is no discernible trend.

We are unable to show the mix for the 1967 and 1970 cohorts because we have no records for individuals in these cohorts who left service before 1977. Limited data on the fraction of blacks, and separately on the fraction of women, in earlier officer accession cohorts are reported in DoD (1998). This data series begins in 1973 with the advent of the All Volunteer Force (AVF). Since it does not report data by occupational group, it is not possible to determine racial and gender diversity among nonprofessionals. However, these data do provide a broad indication of the trends in the early years of the AVF. Between 1973 and 1977, there was a dramatic increase in the diversity of new officer accessions. The fraction of new officers who were black increased from 3 percent to 7 percent, the fraction of Hispanics increased from just over 0 percent to 1 percent, and the fraction of women increased from 8 percent to 14 percent.

As Table 3 shows, however, there are noticeably different levels of diversity and patterns of change in diversity across the military services. The Army and Air Force are more diverse than are the other two services, with each having about one-quarter of their new

---

[4]Unfortunately, the data used for our analysis do not allow us to examine very recent changes in the diversity of the officer corps. Other published data indicate that the proportion of recent officer accessions who are black has risen from 7.4 percent in 1993 to 8.5 percent in 1997, and the proportion who are female has risen from 18.5 percent in 1993 to 19.4 percent in 1997 (Office of the Assistant Secretary of Defense: 1998).

Table 3

Percent of Officer Nonprofessional Accessions by Race and Gender: 1977–91 Cohorts, by Service, and for All Services

	1977	1980	1983	1987	1991
DoD Total					
White Male	82.2%	79.6%	81.2%	82.0%	78.3%
Black Male	6.6	5.3	6.7	5.5	6.1
Other Minority	1.9	2.1	2.0	2.8	4.4
White Female	7.9	11.1	8.0	8.0	9.1
Black Female	1.2	1.6	1.8	1.4	1.4
Other Minority	0.2	0.3	0.3	0.4	0.7
Army					
White Male	76.1%	76.9%	75.3%	73.9%	74.9%
Black Male	8.9	6.3	10.0	10.1	9.2
Other Male	2.7	2.8	1.9	2.5	3.0
White Female	10.3	11.6	9.7	10.1	9.6
Black Female	1.7	1.9	2.8	2.9	2.9
Other Female	0.3	0.4	0.3	0.5	0.5
Navy					
White Male	90.4%	86.3%	87.3%	89.2%	80.4%
Black Male	3.6	3.0	3.1	3.6	5.1
Other Male	1.1	2.1	2.5	2.5	5.4
White Female	4.6	8.1	6.2	4.3	7.6
Black Female	0.3	0.3	0.6	0.3	0.9
Other Female	0.0	0.2	0.3	0.1	0.7
Air Force					
White Male	80.8%	75.8%	81.0%	81.5%	76.7%
Black Male	7.0	6.1	6.2	3.2	4.5
Other Male	1.8	1.8	1.9	3.0	4.6
White Female	8.6	13.5	8.4	10.3	12.2
Black Female	1.6	2.3	2.1	1.3	0.9
Other Female	0.3	0.4	0.4	0.8	1.1
Marine Corps					
White Male	91.6%	91.4%	87.4%	85.7%	86.3%
Black Male	3.9	3.2	6.3	5.6	4.1
Other Male	0.5	0.4	1.8	3.6	5.1
White Female	3.8	4.5	4.3	4.6	3.9
Black Female	0.2	0.4	0.2	0.3	0.2
Other Female	0.0	0.0	0.0	0.1	0.3

NOTES: Excludes officers in professional occupations. Totals may not equal 100 because of rounding error.

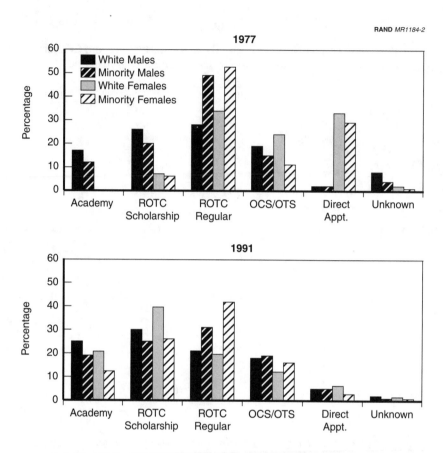

Figure 2—Commissioning Source of Entering Officers
by Race and Gender, 1977 and 1991
(Percent of Minority/Gender Group, Excludes Professional Occupations)

officers belonging to a nonwhite-male group in the 1991 cohort.
There has been little change in the diversity of the Army's officer accessions, if we disregard 1980, which was an anomalous recruiting
year for this service.[5] In contrast, the Air Force has experienced a
decline in black officers, both male and female, and an increase in

---

[5]At this time, low interest in military service due to Vietnam and inadequate pay
caused the services, especially the Army, to have recruiting problems.

the other minority groups. Diversity increased sharply in the Navy between the 1987 and 1991 entering cohorts to just below the Army and Air Force levels; every minority/gender group showed an increase. The least diverse service is the Marine Corps, but the number of other minority males there has increased rapidly in the last ten years.

COMMISSIONING SOURCE AND OCCUPATIONAL ASSIGNMENT

The modest change in racial and gender mix for minority and women officers after 1977 was accompanied by more dramatic changes in the commissioning sources and initial occupations. Most analyses of officer progression, including ours, have found that commissioning source and occupation are factors in retention and promotion.[6] Later in this chapter, when we estimate differences in these important determinants of career progression, we will control for minority/gender differences in the way officers entered into service.

Most of the cohorts we studied entered service during the 1970s and 1980s, when the military was expanding, and early 1990s, when a major drawdown began. As the total number of officer accessions varied—between 12,000 and 20,000—the services changed their use of the different commissioning sources. The services took a disproportionate share of the cut in officer accessions from the regular (nonscholarship) ROTC programs and, to a lesser extent, from the OCS/OTS. The OCS/OTS have produced more or fewer officers as commissioning requirements increased or decreased because of the short lead time between program entry and commissioning.

Figure 2 shows the change in the mix of commissioning sources by race and gender between the earliest cohort we observed at entry, 1977, and the latest cohort whose career progression we studied, 1991. White male officers' commissioning sources shifted to the academies and ROTC scholarship programs and away from OCS/OTS. Before and during the drawdown, minority male officers were considerably more likely than white males to enter through

---

[6]See Bowman (1990), Mehay (1995), and North et al. (1995).

regular ROTC programs, but the overall decline in these programs narrowed this difference. Much more dramatic changes are seen for women officers because the first women graduated from the military academies or with ROTC scholarships in 1980. The differences among women are also more pronounced. In both years, a higher fraction of minority women entered through the regular ROTC program, whereas white women were more likely to enter through OCS/OTS in 1977 and from one of the academies or with an ROTC scholarship in 1991.

Figure 3 examines changes between 1977 and 1991 in the fraction of officers entering with prior service. Between 15 and 25 percent of male officers come from the enlisted ranks, and the racial difference among men in this characteristic is modest (Figure 3). This fraction is smaller for white women, but minority women are as likely as men to have had prior service. In recent years, the commissioning programs for enlisted personnel have increasingly been a source of minority officers.

All the services assign their officers to an occupation before or soon after they are commissioned. However, the personnel records do not record this occupation until the officers complete their occupational training, so we identified the officers' eventual occupations from the fourth-year records. White and minority male officers showed generally similar changes between the 1977 and 1991 cohorts, as there was a shift to tactical, intelligence, and supply occupations and away from maintenance and administrative occupations (Figure 4). Among male officers, minorities were less likely to be in tactical (combat) occupations and more likely to be in supply occupations, and this difference grew somewhat in the later cohort. This difference was greater for black males than for other minority males (not shown). Of course, female officers are considerably less likely to be assigned to tactical occupations, but the easing of the occupation restrictions described in Chapter Two has enabled far more women to enter these fields in recent cohorts. Although the proportion of women in administration has declined over time, so has the proportion of men in administration, and the female-male "gap" has actually grown a little over these cohorts. Finally, the differences between white women and minority women largely mirror the differences between white men and minority men.

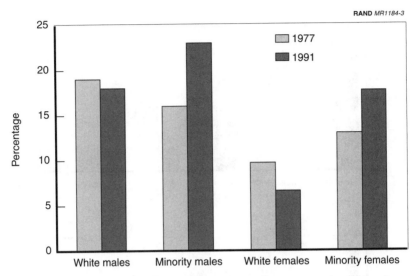

Figure 3—Percent of Entering Officers Who Have Prior Enlisted Service,
1977 and 1991
(Percent of Minority/Gender Group, Excludes Professional Occupations)

MARITAL STATUS

Women officers are considerably less likely than men to be married at all career stages. In our data set, one-half of male officers were married at entry, compared to only one-third for women officers. In the senior ranks (O-5 and O-6), 90 percent of the men and 55 percent of the women were married. Black women were the least likely to marry if they stayed in service. This difference in marital status, and its potential effects on careers, is discussed further in the next chapter.

In conducting our empirical analysis, we had hoped to be able to determine how getting married and having children affect retention and promotion, especially for women officers. However, our data did not allow us to separate the effects of marriage and children from

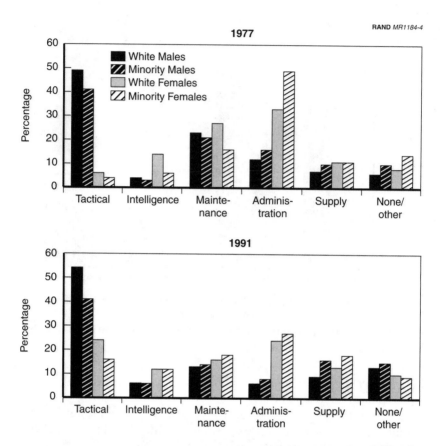

**Figure 4—Distribution of Military Occupations, 1977 and 1991 Cohorts
(Percent of Minority/Gender Group, Excludes Professional Occupations)**

the gender effects beyond the very early stages of the career.[7] To determine the effects of marriage and children on men versus women, we needed to be able to estimate the differences in promotion and retention at each stage for all possible combinations of gender and marital status (or parental status). We could not do this for

---

[7]Married personnel are more likely to be promoted early on, but this effect is smaller for women. Married men are also more likely to be retained, but married women are more likely to leave. See Appendix C for more information on marital status.

several reasons. We could not measure outcomes for single men beyond the early career stages because almost all men marry early in their careers. Even if we could have done this, the data do not tell us who left service to get married or have children. Consequently, we would have treated an officer leaving to get married as the loss of a single officer and failed to detect the connection to marriage. Further, we expect that, even for those whose marital status was correctly identified, retention and marriage decisions are not made independently. Unless these decisions are fully independent, it is not appropriate to include marital status as an explanatory variable in the retention analysis. For all these reasons, we decided to drop any consideration of marital status and number of children in our final data analysis. To the extent that these factors affect women differently than men, they are included in the differences in promotion and retention estimated for women versus men.

DIFFERENCES IN RETENTION AND PROMOTION

We analyzed career progression as a series of retention and promotion outcomes, each conditional on its predecessor. The outcomes are: retention at O-1, promotion to O-2, retention at O-2, promotion to O-3, and so on. So, for example, we analyze promotion to O-3 only for officers who stay through O-1, are promoted at O-2, and stay through O-2. We analyzed nine outcomes:

1. retention at O-1 and promotion to O-2

2. retention at O-2

3. promotion to O-3

4. retention at O-3

5. promotion to O-4

6. retention at O-4

7. promotion to O-5

8. retention at O-5

9. promotion to O-6.

We could not establish separate retention and promotion outcomes for O-1 to O-2 because these happen too quickly to observe through annual records. We include this period in the "promotion" category because the departures often result from failure to perform during training.

The sample used for each of the nine outcomes included all individuals who reached the relevant career stage. An officer who left service at the O-3 retention point would be in the samples for the first four outcomes but not the last five. Since our data were for the years 1977 through 1993, they covered different periods of service for different cohorts, and the retention and promotion outcomes were measured for different subsets of these cohorts. For each outcome, Table 4 shows which cohorts were used for each retention and promotion point.

Determining Retention Outcomes

Earlier, we indicated that determining promotion outcomes was difficult. That is because the data do not record who was considered for promotion. To infer whether individuals were considered for a particular promotion, we looked at whether they stayed in service into

Table 4

Cohorts Used in Analysis of Retention and Promotion at Each Pay Grade

Window	Cohort						
	1967	1970	1977	1980	1983	1987	1991
Retention							
O-2			√	√	√	√	
O-3			√	√			
O-4	√	√	√				
O-5	√	√					
Promotion							
O-1–O-2			√	√	√	√	√
O-2–O-3			√	√	√	√	
O-3–O-4			√	√			
O-4–O-5	√	√					
O-5–O-6	√	√					
Year of Service in Data	10–27	7–24	1–17	1–14	1–11	1–7	1–3

the time interval when others in the same cohort were promoted. These promotions occur over a period of up to three years, which vary by service and cohort. Therefore, we identified a three-year *promotion window* for each grade, cohort, and service based on the distribution of promotions in the data. As an example of how this worked, we defined an individual Army officer as being in the O-4 promotion window if he or she was in service at least the first of the three years others in the same 1977 cohort of Army officers were promoted. This same method was used to identify the other promotion windows for the 1977 Army officer cohort. We then replicated this analysis for the other Army cohorts and the cohorts in each other service. For each cohort and service, we evaluated promotion rates only to those grades for which our data covered the full three-year promotion window.

The years between promotion windows were defined as *retention windows*. Individuals not promoted to a particular grade were not considered to have ever entered the succeeding retention window. For example, officers who were not selected for promotion to O-5 were not included in the sample for the O-5 retention window. Table 5 shows the sample sizes and promotion/retention rates in the sample that resulted from this analysis. Note that, although we have combined the charts and services in Table 5, separate windows were defined for each cohort in each service.

Table 5

Sample Size and Promotion/Retention Rate by Pay Grade

Window	Sample Size	Percent Retained/Promoted
Retention		
O-2	61,837	92.1%
O-3	25,028	64.6
O-4	17,556	89.3
O-5	8,465	68.5
Promotion		
O-1–O-2	76,337	95.3%
O-2–O-3	56,926	87.9
O-3–O-4	16,176	74.6
O-4–O-5	10,619	73.6
O-5–O-6	5,800	50.2

Figure 5 again combines the data for all cohorts and services to show the average timing of career windows and the average fraction of the entering cohorts we studied who remained in the military at the end of each window. Since officers who fail to make a promotion are not counted in the next window even if they stay, Figure 5 looks somewhat different than the usual year-of-service (YOS) cohort profile, which includes these individuals until they actually leave.

Method for Estimating Differences

For each of the nine windows, we estimated the difference in the fraction retained or promoted between white male officers and up to five minority/gender groups, depending on sample sizes: black men, other minority men, white women, black women, and other minority women. This is different from other studies we are aware of, which typically have estimated differences for whites versus minorities and for men versus women, but not for groups defined by race/ethnicity *and* gender.

We used logistic regressions to separate the effects of race and gender from the other factors measured in the cohort data file, such as

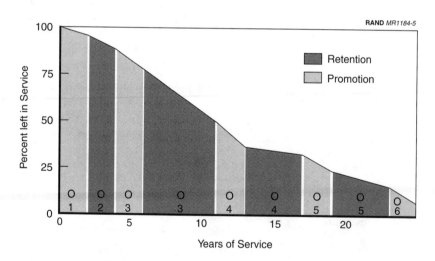

Figure 5—Average Profile of Officer Cohorts Studied

commissioning source, prior enlisted service, and military occupation. We should note here that the effects of other factors that might
be correlated with the outcomes we analyzed were not measured in
the cohort data file (e.g., individual aptitude, quality of undergraduate education, and physical fitness are not controlled for in our
model). To the extent that these unmeasured factors systematically
differ for minority and female officers, their effects will be included
in the retention and promotion differences we estimated for these
groups of officers.

Estimation Results

Figures 6–8 display the estimated differences in the completion rates
for black and other minority males, white females, and black and
other minority females while holding constant the other variables in
the model. These other variables are:

- whether the person had prior enlisted service;

- military service;

- accession source: academy, ROTC scholarship, ROTC regular,
  OCS/OTS, direct appointment, unknown accession source;

- occupation: executive, intelligence, engineering and maintenance, administration, supply/procurement, other; and

- cohort: varies by promotion or retention window.

The figures show the differences between the groups of minority
and/or female officers and white male officers in the fractions who
complete the retention and promotion windows.[8] For example, the
+7 percent estimate in Figure 6 means that the percentage of black
males who complete the O-3 retention window is 7 points higher
than the percentage of white males who complete the same window.
Again, these results are for officers who are not in a profession such
as medicine.

---

[8]These estimates are transformed from the logistic regression coefficients by evaluat-
ing the expression $\bar{p}_i(1-\bar{p}_i)\beta_i$, where $\bar{p}_i$ is the average fraction in all relevant cohorts
progressing through the ith window and β_i is the coefficient from the logistic
regression that measures the difference in the fraction for a minority/gender group.

Figure 6 presents the results for black men in all career windows and for other minority men through the O-4 retention window (beyond this point, the sample size was too small to estimate their outcomes). Generally, minority men are more likely than white men to stay in

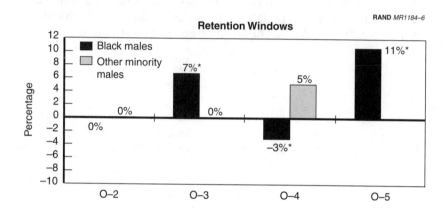

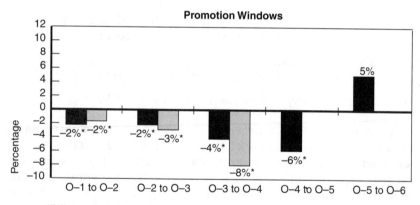

*Differences that are significant at .05 level.

Figure 6—Differences in Completion Rates for Minority Male vs. White Male Officers

service between promotion periods.[9] The one exception to this is after promotion to O-4, when black men are slightly less likely to remain. Some of the officers who leave at this point have had prior enlisted service and have reached the 20-year retirement point. Although slightly more black officers have prior enlisted service and might leave at this point, our analysis controls for this difference. We were not able to determine what other factors might be contributing as well.

In contrast, all groups of minority men are consistently less likely than white men to successfully pass through promotion windows. The pattern of negative differences is broken, however, at promotion to O-6. By this point, the remaining officers have all compiled records of consistently superior performance. Also, the sample for analyzing the O-6 promotion window was very small since it included officers who were commissioned in 1967 and 1970, when entering cohorts were far less diverse.

The lower promotion rates largely counteract the higher retention rates for black men. Thus, combining promotion and retention differences, we find that there is almost no difference between black and white male officers in the likelihood of getting from O-1 to O-4, the first field-grade rank. Of those who are commissioned, only 1 percent fewer black men make O-4—a difference that is not statistically significant. The same cannot be said for other minority men; 6 percent fewer of them than white men reach O-4 rank.

In the early stages of their careers (before O-4), white women are less likely to stay during retention periods and somewhat less likely than white men to be promoted (Figure 7). The differences generally become positive at the O-4 point. There are two possible explanations for the contrast between the pre–O-4 and post–O-4 results for white women. First, there could have been a shift in the behavior and performance of women who entered in the cohorts after 1980 since these cohorts are included only in the pre–O-4 analysis. Second, it may be the case that women who do not choose to actively pursue a military career fall out before the field grades and the women who remain are more committed. Since we were unable to detect any dif-

---

[9]The lower retention rates estimated for other minorities at O-3 are statistically significant only in the uncontrolled model.

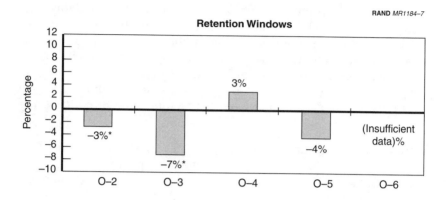

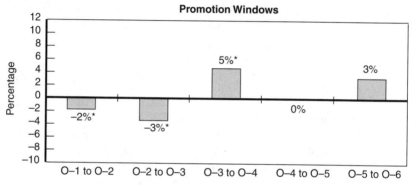

*Differences that are significant at .05 level.

**Figure 7—Differences in Completion Rates for White
Female vs. White Male Officers**

ferences in the cohorts that would explain this result, we are left with
the second explanation.

Career progression for minority women generally resembles career
progression for minority men (Figure 8), with a higher retention rate
for black women at the rank of O-3 and lower completion rates in all
promotion windows through O-4. The sample of minority women
above the O-4 promotion point is increasingly small, so we were not
able to obtain results for the later career windows.

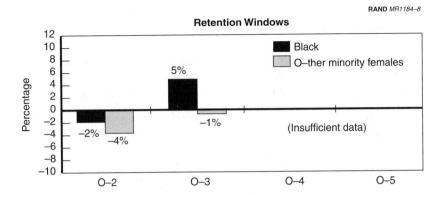

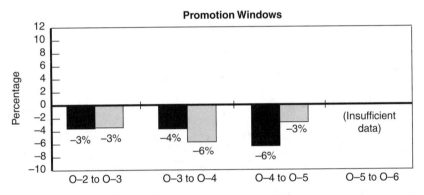

*Differences from rate of white males that are significant at .05 level.

**Figure 8—Differences in Completion Rates for Minority Female
vs. White Male Officers**

Minority/Gender Differences Not Controlling for Entry Path

Source of commission, prior service, and occupation significantly affected the probability of progressing through most of the retention and promotion windows (see regression results in Appendix C). The results we presented above control for these other factors, so we can conclude that the racial and gender differences we found are not attributable to racial and gender differences in commissioning source, prior service, or occupation. It is possible that there are further racial/gender differences in career progression that are caused by the differences in these entry attributes, but that these differences are masked by the multivariate approach we used for this analysis. To see whether there are indirect effects due to source of commission, prior service, and occupation, we reanalyzed the data and omitted these attributes. We will call these the "unadjusted" results.

We did not find any evidence of additional indirect effects due to these factors. Where the estimated differences between minorities or women and white males change at all, the change is very modest. For example, the gaps in completion of the promotion windows for black males are slightly larger in the unadjusted results (–5.6 vs. –4.2 percentage points for the O-4 promotion window). Thus, our findings cannot be explained by the differences in source of commission, prior service, and occupation for minority and female officers compared to white male officers.

Minority and Gender Differences by Service and Cohort

In carrying out our analysis, we looked for evidence that career progression for minorities and women has differed across services or cohorts. Does one service have a better or worse record than the other services? Is there evidence of a trend toward more equal progression over time?

The results of our service- and cohort-specific analyses are summarized in Appendix C. Our results did vary across services and cohorts. However, there was no consistent pattern to the variations, a conclusion supported by the formal statistical tests we carried out.

Summary of Retention and Promotion Results

To summarize the racial and gender differences we found, we calculated how many officers out of an entering group of 100 would be lost from the pipeline and whether they were lost in a retention or promotion window (Table 6). We focused on the results for whites and blacks because these are based on larger samples than the results for other minorities. The bottom line is that women are less likely to reach field grade than are men, but within the genders there are no racial differences in this outcome. *How* officers leave does vary by

Table 6

**Comparison of Losses Between Commissioning and O-4
by Race and Gender**

	White Men	Black Men	White Women	Black Women
Initial Count	100	100	100	100
Number who leave during retention	35	28	40	30
Number who leave during promotion	28	36	30	39
Number who remain to O-4	37	36	30	31

race, however. White men and white women are more likely to leave than are black men and women during periods when their departure is likely to be voluntary. Black men and women are considerably more likely to leave at a promotion point.

The differences are even clearer if we look at the relative likelihoods of leaving for the two reasons, voluntary departure versus promotion failure. We will illustrate the calculation of these relative odds using the example of black men versus white men. During retention windows before O-4, Table 6 shows that, out of an initial count of 100 in both groups, 28 black men will leave and 35 white men will leave. We calculate that the likelihood of a black man leaving is 20 percent less than the likelihood of a white man leaving because $(.28-.35)/.35 = -.20$. Figure 9 plots the relative differences in retention and promotion for black men, white women, and black women. In simple terms, compared to white men:

- Black men are more likely to stay in the service between promotions but are less likely to be promoted.

- White women are less likely to stay in the service between promotions and are slightly less likely to be promoted.

- Black women are more likely to stay in the service between promotions but are less likely to be promoted.

When all three groups we describe here are compared, black men are least likely to choose to leave the service and white women are most likely to choose to leave. All three groups are less likely to be

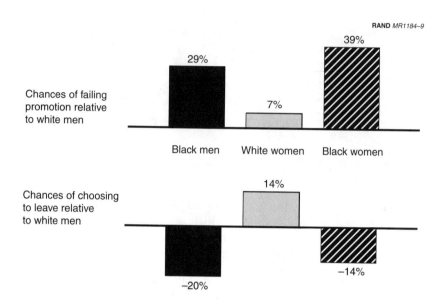

**Figure 9—Retention vs. Promotion of Black and Female Officers
Through O-4, Relative to White Male Officers**

promoted than are white men, but this discrepancy is smaller for white women than it is for black men and women.

Our promotion results are consistent with other studies conducted in recent years of officer promotion in the Navy and Marine Corps. Mehay (1995) has found that black naval surface officers and Marine officers were less likely to be selected for O-4 promotion between 1985 and 1990. North et al. (1995) have estimated that, between 1987 and 1993, black Marine officers scored lower at TBS, were less likely to be augmented to a regular commission, and were less likely to be selected for promotion to O-3 and O-4. Hispanic and female officers did as well as white officers on most measures. An older study of Naval Academy graduates (Bowman, 1990) has concluded that black graduates from 1976 to 1980 were more likely than white graduates to stay beyond their initial obligation and less likely to rate in the top half of all graduates on their early performance evaluations. Therefore, in turning to our interviews and focus groups, we were most interested in obtaining officers' opinions about why black men and women are less likely to complete promotion windows and white women are less likely to complete retention windows than are white men. Our estimates of promotion and retention rates adjust for the effects of commissioning source, prior service, and military occupation as well as service and cohort. These were the factors measured in our data. The other research cited above has used more detailed service data and found that other factors also are important. The most extensive set of factors have been evaluated by Mehay; he has found that officers who graduated from more competitive institutions of higher learning, majored in technical subjects, and had higher grades received more positive performance evaluations that led directly to higher promotion rates to lieutenant commander (O-4). Although fewer minority officers than white officers came from competitive colleges or had good grades, controlling for these differences did not explain the lower evaluation ratings and promotion rates for black officers.

Chapter Four

OFFICERS' PERCEPTIONS OF RACIAL DIFFERENCES IN CAREER PROGRESSION

In the last chapter, we found that black officers are more likely than white officers to separate at times of promotion. Black officers are also less likely to leave voluntarily in between promotions.[1] To better understand why this difference exists, this chapter draws on the project's extensive semistructured one-on-one and group interviews. We present the common *perceptions* offered by the officers in these discussions as to why career progression differs for blacks.

Blacks and whites offer distinct and often contradictory explanations for group differences in career progress. Each of these explanations for differences in the career progress of blacks should not be interpreted simply as fact; they are the *perceptions* of members of these groups. Perceptions are important in that they represent how members of each group interpret their experiences in the career-management system; however, an individual's perception of an interaction may be inaccurate if he or she misjudges the motives or assumptions of other individuals in the interaction.[2] As one black female officer stated: "When there is a personality conflict, it's always hard to say what caused it. Do they hate officers [from my

---

[1]We found similar differences for other minority males and females. However, as discussed elsewhere, the sample sizes for these groups were too small for precise measurement of retention and promotion differences, and the bases we visited had too few of these officers for the focus groups discussed in this chapter and the next one.

[2]For research demonstrating how race can affect the meaning individuals ascribe to the actions of others in an interaction, see Hamilton and Trolier (1986), Inman and Baron (1996), and Poskocil (1977).

occupation field]? Or is it because I'm female or black or from [a southern state]?" In a similar vein, a white officer commented, "It's tough to confront minorities without it possibly being interpreted as being a racial thing." Where possible, we also discuss other evidence, both from our research and the research of others, that supports or refutes individuals' perceptions. Chapter Five presents a similar discussion regarding the perceptions of gender difference in career progression.

Except where stated otherwise, the issues presented in this chapter apply equally to both black men and women officers. Black women did not raise any issues in our discussions that were not also discussed by either black men or white women. Issues related to gender for black women will be discussed in the next chapter. Perceptions generically attributed to white officers in this chapter indicate perceptions that were expressed by both white men and women in our discussions. Our conversations with white women focused primarily on gender issues; as a consequence, some racial issues were discussed with white males but not with white females. Where we had little basis to assert that white women concurred or disagreed with comments by white males, we have attributed the perspective only to white males. Therefore, readers should note that white women did not necessarily disagree with perspectives attributed to white males.

ANALYTIC APPROACH

A complete description of who was interviewed and how the interviews were conducted can be found in Appendix D, but a brief explication of our analytic approach is warranted here. We interviewed three sets of individuals: officers with duties to manage aspects of officer careers (primarily detailers and assignment officers, training personnel, officers who organize and assist promotion boards, and officers responsible for officer policy on headquarters staffs); senior officers who have recently sat on boards deciding promotions to O-5 and O-6; and midcareer officers (O-3 and O-4). These three groups were selected to help us understand how the officer career and promotion system is supposed to run and how the system is perceived to run. In total, we interviewed 233 officers:

- 45 career managers,

- 45 promotion board members,

- 143 midcareer officers.

We conducted one-on-one or small group interviews with career managers that were exploratory and unstructured in nature. These interviews were part of the study team's initial exercise to learn the basics of how officer careers progress. Most of the information from these interviews appeared in Chapter Two, which described officer career-management policies and practices. Our discussions with recent promotion board members took place as semistructured focus groups, according to a loosely scripted protocol.[3] The protocol focused on the process followed during board deliberations and what distinguishes successful candidates. We allowed discussions to deviate considerably from the protocol when they took an informative turn.

We held interviews and focus groups with midcareer officers as part of our site visits to one major installation from each service. The RAND study team provided each base with detailed specifications regarding how discussion participants were to be selected.[4] In general, we selected participants from each racial/gender group to ensure representation from the full range of occupational specialties and commissioning sources.

We conducted one-on-one interviews with roughly one-quarter of the midcareer officers in our sample; the rest we interviewed in focus groups. Table 7 presents the racial and gender background of the midcareer officers we interviewed. As with the promotion board focus groups, both the one-on-one and focus group discussions with midcareer officers were conducted using semistructured protocols.[5] Again, we allowed discussions to deviate from the protocol when they took an informative tack.

---

[3]Protocols for the promotion board focus groups can be found in Appendix C.

[4]See Appendix C for a detailed description of the selection criteria.

[5]Protocols for the one-on-one interviews and focus groups with midcareer officers can be found in Appendix C. We used the protocols as a general guide for the discussions and to ensure that each focus group addressed all the key issues.

Table 7

Racial and Gender Background of Midcareer
Officers in Our Discussions

Race/Gender	Proportion of the Officers Interviewed
White Men	0.29
Black Men	0.29
White Women	0.27
Black Women	0.15
Total	1.00

With the midcareer officers, we conducted separate focus groups for black males, white males, black females, and white females in order to provide an environment for discussion in which people felt free to express opinions and share experiences. The RAND interview teams were mixed along both racial and gender lines and had substantial diversity with regard to academic discipline, military research experience, and personal military service.[6] To begin each focus group, participants described their career experiences. This was followed by a more general discussion of important aspects such as occupational assignment, duty assignment, performance evaluation, promotion, and retention. Many focus groups brought up issues related to race and gender during this discussion. If these issues did not arise, the interview team asked about minorities and women at the end of the general discussion.

We did not video or audio tape any of the discussions in order to minimize subjects' protection concerns and because we felt taping might inhibit some from fully participating in a discussion. Interviewers kept general notes during one-on-one conversations then transcribed the notes shortly after the interview. Each focus group employed a dedicated note taker who kept a detailed record of

---

[6]Logistically, it was not possible for us to always match the race/gender of a focus group discussion leader to that of the discussion group's participants. This might have biased our data toward an understatement of perceived racial differences, as prior studies have shown that in responding to a white interviewer, blacks tend to underplay expressions of racial differences in experiences or attitudes (see Anderson et al., 1988; Davis, 1997). Similar behavior is expected with white responses to a black interviewer (Hatchett and Schuman, 1975–76).

the group discussion. While this prevented us from compiling verbatim transcripts of the discussions, our notes are quite detailed, and we feel they serve as a solid basis from which to determine the relative emphasis participants placed on various issues and concerns.

The semistructured discussion format and the nature of our notes limited our ability to apply a formal content analysis to the interview transcripts. To ensure that our analysis was as careful as possible, several members of the study team independently reviewed the discussion notes. Each person evaluated the relative importance that each racial/gender group placed on a specified set of issues, and the study team reviewed the separate evaluations. The findings reported in this chapter are the result of that process.

Throughout this chapter we employ only broad descriptive adjectives to characterize the relative level of agreement with a perception or concern. Unlike survey methods, qualitative interviewing methods are not designed to strictly quantify the proportion of participants who adhere to a particular opinion. Instead, this chapter and the next build on the strength of qualitative data, providing a rich understanding of complex attitudes and relationships. Qualitative data analysis is particularly useful for developing hypotheses about the reasons for patterns revealed in quantitative data gathered from the same setting.[7]

Most of the information we report is taken from the focus groups and interviews with midcareer officers. Occasionally, we refer to comments made by either career managers or promotion board members. To ensure that the source is clear, we refer to each group as follows:

- "midcareer officers" or "officers,"

- "officer career managers" or "managers,"

- "promotion board members" or "board members."

---

[7]For a discussion of the strengths and weaknesses of qualitative data analysis, see Miles and Huberman (1994) or Rubin and Rubin (1995).

COMPETITIVENESS OF PERFORMANCE OR BIAS IN THE CAREER-MANAGEMENT SYSTEM

Most midcareer white officers whom we interviewed stated that they expected no meaningful differences between the career progression of black and white officers.[8] By and large, they did not believe that black officers are disadvantaged in their career progression because of their race.

The consensus among the white male officers in our discussions was that career success and promotion are driven by performance only. One white officer succinctly stated, "Performance is all that matters." The following exchange from a focus group with promotion board members further supports this view:

> *Interviewer:* What makes a candidate competitive for promotion?
> *Board member 1:* A sustained manner of performance. Not just one report.
> *Board member 2:* That's the only real absolute. You can compensate for bad assignments, but you must have sustained demonstrated performance.

This meritocratic view of the career-management system implies that race or gender, in and of itself, does not affect an officer's success. As one officer stated, "My experience is that good officers get promoted and they get the good jobs. You get promoted for ability, not race or sex. I've never seen good minority officers or women officers not get jobs if they were good." The presence of black officers at the highest ranks in the services—Colin Powell for example—was often offered as proof against discrimination in the system.

Some white male officers went a step further in challenging the notion that black males are disadvantaged in the career-management system. These officers believed that it is white officers

------

[8]It is possible that white officers expressed an expectation of no meaningful racial differences because they thought this to be the most appropriate response, rather than what they actually believed. For highly charged issues, such as abortion, race, or homosexuality, responses to interview or survey questions can be particularly sensitive to social norms, as the expression of actual beliefs can embarrass respondents or a group with which they are affiliated (Dovidio and Fazio, 1992).

who are at a disadvantage in the career-management system. They offered as proof of this advantage the promotion goals of board precepts and other personnel policies that explicitly treated minorities and women differently.

As we described above, during the interviews RAND researchers informed officers that differences could be seen in the career progression of black officers without expressing the nature of these differences.[9] Three primary themes emerged in the explanations offered by white male officers for any racial differences in rated performance.[10] These officers felt that:

- On average, black officers enter with weaker skills and abilities; in particular, historically black colleges and universities do not prepare students well for the rigorous demands of an officer's career.

- Black officers tend to separate themselves socially and don't work as hard to develop the peer and mentoring relationships that are critically important to an officer's success.

- Civilian employers aggressively recruit black officers in an effort to meet their own affirmative action goals, and some blacks use the military as a stepping stone to a good civilian job explicitly because of its equitable treatment of minorities.

---

[9]Discussion leaders initially asked participants whether they thought racial or gender differences existed in the career progress of officers. In those discussions where participants stated that they thought no differences existed, discussion leaders then asserted that administrative data showed differences do exist, without indicating to participants which group was disadvantaged. Discussion leaders then again asked participants to identify what differences they might expect and why they developed. If after further discussion, the participants continued to identify the wrong group as disadvantaged, the discussion leader would assert the correct findings from the administrative data and ask the participants to again comment on why they thought such differences occurred.

[10]It is common for those who are successful to believe that an evaluation system is based on merit, and for those who fail to blame their lack of success on unfair treatment (Saal and Moore, 1993; Sherman et al., 1983). Evaluators tend to set lower minimum competency standards and higher standards for demonstrated ability for women and minorities; thus, these groups find it harder to prove their performance is based on ability (Biernat and Kobrynowicz, 1997).

Thus, the common thread that ran through our discussions with white male officers was their overwhelming rejection of the notion that black officers are systematically disadvantaged in the career-management system. Instead, an individual black officer's failure to attain senior rank was attributed directly to factors such as his or her preference for civilian life or weaknesses in his or her skills and abilities.[11]

Nearly all black officers in our discussions concurred with the expressed belief among white officers that job performance, and its recognition, are the primary drivers of an officer's success. As one black officer stated, "To get promoted, you need good performance in the right jobs." By and large, the black officers we interviewed accepted the fairness of the promotion board deliberations, given the information that is presented to the board. Further, black officers rejected the notion that they received an advantage in the process. Instead, most of them expressed a belief that factors other than an individual's ability often affect the evaluation and recognition of a black officer's performance. Thus, nearly all black officers in our discussions expected that the measured career progress of blacks would be weaker than the progress of their white peers.

In general, black officers raised three issues that they believe limit their ability to develop competitive career records for promotion boards to consider:

- White officers expect black officers to have weaker skills and abilities; to overcome this expectation, the "performance bar" gets increased for black officers.

- Cultural barriers make it harder for black officers to develop the strong peer and mentor relationships that provide access to information and resources necessary for career success.

- Black officers are less likely to get career-enhancing assignments or be selected for participation in important missions.

---

[11]Kluegel (1990) asserts that whites have increasingly come to ascribe the primary cause of racial differences to differences in educational attainment and individual personality characteristics, rather than to inequities in a stratification system. This "allows privileged whites to avoid blame for the gap while endorsing an explanation commonly viewed as unprejudiced" (p. 523).

Thus, most officers, black and white, accepted the basic fairness with which promotion boards review the records of black officers. A broad consensus existed in our discussions that the difficulties black officers have in their career development lie in establishing competitive performance records. The issues raised in our discussions with blacks and whites to explain these difficulties were: precommissioning preparation, skills, and abilities; social integration and the formation of peer and mentor relationships; assignment patterns; and competing opportunities. The remainder of this chapter summarizes the discussions on these issues and the issue of bias in favor of black officers.

PRECOMMISSIONING PREPARATION AND SKILLS

A clear parallel existed in the discussions among black and white officers regarding the precommissioning preparation, skills, and abilities of black officers. Nearly all white officers expressed a belief that promotion and career success are driven by performance; therefore, most white officers concluded that the promotion failure of individual black officers necessarily derives from their weaker performance. The cause of this weaker performance is seen as stemming from weaker skills, abilities, or precommissioning preparation of the particular black officer. "The service has lowered standards to admit more minorities, so of course they look worse than whites," stated one white officer. Another stated that the services are "bending over backwards to keep unqualified officers in."

Black officers clearly perceived this attitude to be widespread among white officers. Many black officers in our discussions believed that in each new situation, others assume them to be less capable. "Some people automatically expect [of blacks] some things, intellectually, athletically. They expect these across the board," commented one black officer. Another black officer commented:

> People question your ability for basic oral and written skills, especially if you come from a historically black university. It used to piss me off to get "you speak well." I think I am supposed to be on a peer level with them. . . . Small white colleges are thought to be okay, especially small white military colleges. Whereas, if I'm black, I am not expected to speak and write as well.

Some black officers expressed a sense that white officers are quick to judge all black officers on the failings of any one black officer. One officer commented, "It also depends on the guy there before you. Say there was a minority officer who didn't do a good job. Then they put other minorities in the same category when they come along."

Many black officers whom we interviewed felt that their successes are not given the same attention as their failures. These black officers believed that others attribute a black officer's success to the service's affirmative action efforts, rather than to his or her skills and abilities. As one black officer commented:

> What gets me even more is that when we do make it, it's assumed that we have done so because we are token, or that we got there through affirmative action, not because we were the best at our job. But if you are put in a position and you are white, the issue of why you are there is never questioned.

As a result, most black officers felt that they must constantly prove themselves capable, while other officers are assumed capable until they prove otherwise. A black officer observed, "I have to work twice as hard as the next person. I cannot be average."

That said, some black officers in our discussions acknowledged their belief that the services do bring in a number of blacks with weaker skills and preparation. Commenting on the ROTC programs at historically black colleges, one officer stated, "If ROTC programs would force more English and writing, it would be a big help." A different black officer offered, "Sometimes people get rushed and are not ready for prime time and fall on their face."

We examined outside sources to expand upon this belief. DoD-wide data sources do not contain information for assessing officers' precommissioning preparation. The limited research on this issue is based on Navy and Marine Corps data. These data indicate, on average, that black officers tend to receive their bachelor's degree from colleges that are less competitive than those attended by their white peers (North and Smith, 1993; Mehay, 1995). Black Marine Corps officer candidates are more likely than white candidates to receive aptitude score waivers[12] and subsequently perform less well during TBS training (North et al., 1994; North and Smith, 1993).

A few studies have examined career outcomes after controlling for measures of performance or precommissioning preparation. North et al. (1995) have controlled for TBS performance scores, general classification test scores, and completion of various professional military education courses in estimating chances of promotion to Captain and Major among Marine officers. These background and preparation measures have not explained why black males were substantially less likely to be promoted to Captain and Major than were their white peers in fiscal years 1987–93.

In contrast to North et al., in a study of unrestricted line Navy officers, Mehay (1995) has found that controlling for college GPA and type of degree reduces the racial difference in chances of promotion from O-3 to O-4 by more than 50 percent. When Mehay added a control for ratings given on performance evaluation reports, the racial difference in promotion chances became statistically insignificant. This finding supports the belief among the officers participating in this study that promotion board decisions fairly reflect officers' performance evaluations. However, because the performance evaluations are subjective evaluations of officers' performance, they could reflect any systematic biases regarding minority officers by raters.

SOCIAL SEPARATION

Peer and mentor relationships are seen as key to an officer's career success. They can provide access to information and resources that enhance an officer's performance as well as the recognition received for this performance. One officer noted, "One learns the key things, but the nuances come from peers." An exchange between two black officers in one of the focus groups carried a similar thought: (Officer

---

[12]Officer candidates in the Marine Corps are required to have a minimum combined SAT score of 1,000. An officer candidate with lower scores can be admitted only if he or she receives an aptitude waiver. It should be noted that the relationship between aptitude test score and performance as an officer is by no means clear. Analysis by the Center for Naval Analysis has found no relationship between aptitude test scores and promotion to Captain and Major. (North et al., 1994)

1) "If you did not have the gouge,[13] you were in trouble. Most blacks were not in that clique. . . ." (Officer 2) "The gouge is a subjective process that we get shut out of." Most of the black officers we interviewed felt that at one time or another, they had been shut out of social interactions. One officer commented, "There were also some functions that [my peers] didn't invite me to (I was the only one not invited). We get shut out of some of the information flow because we don't socialize with the others as much." Yet some acknowledged that at times blacks also separate themselves from socializing with their peers:

> A lot of minority officers choose not to participate. I have met blacks who have chosen not to socialize. . . . I have also met whites who chose not to socialize. It has a greater impact on blacks though. There are so few that it is noticed when you are not there.

There was a consensus regarding the value of mentors. As one officer observed, "If you have a mentor, you will go places, to better assignments, and assignments make or break a career. Two equal guys in equal assignments can go up or down on mentors." Yet many black officers in our discussions felt that it was less common for senior officers to mentor young black officers. "The biggest hang-up in finding a mentor is that the [commanding officer] has to see himself as a young [junior officer] in you. [White officers] don't see us that way," commented one black officer.[14]

---

[13]The gouge is a Navy slang term used to describe the informal assistance that officers receive from their peers. An example might be trading information such as old class notes or telling a new shipmate about the Captain's personal preferences regarding ship operations.

[14]Social research has long argued that mentors are an important factor in determining an individual's success in an organization (Dreher and Ash, 1990; Fagenson, 1989; Kanter, 1977; Kram, 1985; Thomas, 1990). Recent research has begun to focus particular attention on racial and gender differences in the chances of developing mentoring relations and the structures that such relationships take. In some settings, blacks have been found to be less likely to form mentoring relationships (Cox and Nkomo, 1991) while in others there has been no significant difference in the chances of forming mentoring relationships (Dreher and Cox, 1996).

The context and meaning of mentoring relationships can also be different for blacks and whites. Cross-race mentor relationships have been found to provide less psychosocial support than same race relationships (Thomas, 1990). Yet because white men tend to occupy more senior positions in organizations, the advantage received

Peer and mentor relationships are viewed as an integral component of an officer's job, not just as important for his or her access to resources. One officer said, "You need to interact; if you don't socialize, you are an outsider, not a team player." Another officer offered, "Part of being an officer is socializing with each other, building unit cohesion, esprit, so some [socializing with your peers] is mandatory."

Black officers in our discussions expressed a clear sense that it is harder for them to fit into the culture of the officer corps than it is for their white peers. They perceived the culture of the officer corps to be unmistakably white and middle class. Commenting on the difficulties of fitting into the military culture, one officer stated, "You need to avoid 'black' mannerisms—speech, walk—because the first impression is very important." Echoes of this perspective were heard in the interviews with white officers; one white officer commented, "If people start walking around with different 'chains,' you may perceive the person is not part of the unit or doesn't want to be." Another white officer commented, "The ones that have the *Ebony* and *Jet* magazines out and get together with black enlisted personnel, they create a counterculture of their own making."

Other black officers recognized that the nature of the social situation is not always so clear. A senior black officer noted, "Perception is reality to young minorities. The reality may be that they are not excluded, but that is their perception." Yet young black officers with little experience interacting in such an environment can feel it difficult both to be accepted in and to accept this setting. A black promotion board member offered the following observation:

> Anyone at lower social class than middle class feels less entitled. So they don't think that the door is open. When there is, for instance, a "Hail and Farewell" to a captain, he or she has never seen parents who have done that type of socializing, so they exclude themselves from what should be fun. They think they will get ahead purely by hard work, but it is relationships that do it. It's who trusts you. So they keep their nose to the grindstone, but they don't participate.

---

from being mentored can be higher with white male mentors than mentors from other demographic groups (Dreher and Cox, 1996).

Some black midcareer officers indicated that it could be as difficult to find support and guidance from other black officers as it is to find support and guidance from the broader officer community.[15] One black officer noted:

> We don't know how to mentor each other. . . . [There] was a black female high-ranking officer, and she had never had a meeting with other black females, had never been to a NNOA[16] conference. It was a big deal that she was a Captain, but she never associated with other blacks. . . . When I called her, I figured she is a Captain, she is black, she has the gouge, she will steer me right. But she did nothing. We don't know how to mentor.

Many black officers in our discussions perceived that others take notice when blacks socialize together, seeing this as an act of separatism. In that vein, a white officer commented that "the only thing that I've seen is a tendency with a small group of minority officers to hang out together." [17] The impression is that black officers feel that it is uncomfortable for a group of black officers to talk together. A black officer commented, "People will look at you because there are four of us sitting there talking and it's a problem! Everybody gravitates to people like them. But it's okay if 50 white guys are talking together." As a result, black officers sometimes avoid gathering to talk, even though they would like to. Another black officer observed:

> You need a minority looking out for you, but even they get sucked up in the system and do not want to be seen as taking care of other black officers. We cannot openly take care of each other. If we do, we are seen as being prejudiced.

---

[15]There is considerably less social research on who mentors than on who is mentored. Yet there are references in some general writings by black men about the difficulty of mentoring other blacks without being seen as favoring blacks (Jones, 1986; Feagin and Sikes, 1994).

[16]National Naval Officers' Association, an association of naval officers who are predominantly black.

[17]There is ample evidence that in many settings, for example, integrated schools, personal friendships, or church membership, individuals socially self-segregate along racial or gender characteristics (Hallinan, 1982; Whitley et al., 1984; and Metz, 1986).

Unfortunately, there are no aggregate data available to evaluate whether black officers on the whole have greater difficulty forming peer and mentor relationships. The 1992 Survey of Officer and Enlisted Personnel (SOEP) does show that black officers are somewhat less satisfied with their coworkers, but it also shows no significant racial differences in an officer's perception of support from his or her supervisors (see Figure 11).[18]

ASSIGNMENTS

In our interviews many black officers expressed a sense that they are often shut out of career-enhancing assignments. Many black officers felt that others' expectations about their skills and abilities and the difficulties they experience forming peer and mentor relationships limited their opportunities to get important career-enhancing assignments or to be selected for important missions. One white assignment officer commented that, in making duty assignments, "When it comes down to two people who look the same on paper, it will come down to further input about personal relations. Detailers[19] used to log who would call regarding a particular officer." A black officer commented:

> Sometimes it is very hard [for minorities] to get the job—like being a black quarterback—no matter how good you are, no matter how hard you kick, scream, or beg, you still will not get the job. You are always placed in the safety position. You don't have many options, and that gets you passed over.

Broader evidence of this *perception* can be found in the 1992 SOEP. White officers, in contrast, were somewhat more likely than black officers to perceive that they were in a career-enhancing assignment (see Figure 11).[20]

---

[18]The difference between black men and white men and between black women and white women in satisfaction with one's coworkers is significant at the .05 level. The racial differences in perceived support from one's supervisors are not significant at the .05 level.

[19]A detailer is an officer who makes assignment decisions in the Navy.

[20]The difference between black men and white men and between black women and white women in whether one's current assignment will help in promotion is significant at the .05 level.

Black officers' ability to develop competitive career records may also be aggravated by policies that the services have developed to increase the number of minority recruits. In discussions with officer managers and midcareer officers, we were told that the services place minority officers disproportionately in certain positions: recruiting and ROTC assignments, where they have high visibility to potential minority recruits, and the Equal Opportunity (EO) Office. Unfortunately, many officers regard these assignments as less desirable than assignments in their career field. These assignments take officers out of their particular occupational fields for a period of time, potentially weakening their ability to demonstrate "occupational credibility" in their career profile. Thus, while these policies may increase the services' ability to recruit and retain minorities, they may simultaneously damage the long-term competitiveness of black officers for promotion. This is despite the fact that all services explicitly instruct promotion board members that atypical assignment patterns among minorities and women may be due to the services' assignment policies, rather than a reflection of the caliber of the officer.

We could not independently assess whether blacks are less likely to receive career-enhancing or damaging assignments; the information on job assignments in the administrative records available to us was too limited to distinguish such positions. However, a recent GAO study (1995) of a limited number of high-profile, career-enhancing jobs in the Army, Navy, and Air Force found no significant difference in the relative chances of receiving such assignments between white and black officers. It should be noted that the GAO study did not examine the relative chances of assignment to positions thought to be career damaging. However, the Army's Office of Economic and Manpower Analysis has reported that black officers are twice as likely as white officers to be serving in a recruiting assignment, although black officers appear no more likely to be serving in ROTC commands.[21]

---

[21]Original calculations conducted by the Office of Economic and Manpower Analysis for RAND based on the March 1997 Army Officer Master File.

COMPETING OPPORTUNITIES

In our discussions, white officers frequently stated that black officers disproportionately choose to leave the military to pursue civilian careers. White officers offered two explanations for this phenomenon. First, civilian companies "bid off" black officers from the military to fulfill their own affirmative action goals. Second, black officers are believed to use the military as a stepping stone to a good civilian job, never intending to pursue a full military career.

Black officers emphatically rejected the notion that they are using military service as a stepping stone to civilian employment. They also did not believe that their civilian opportunities were better than those of other officers. It is also worth noting that many black officers in our discussions expressed the belief that any disadvantages that they have experienced during their military career probably would also occur if they chose to work for a civilian employer.

If black officers were leaving to pursue civilian opportunities, we would expect to see higher losses between promotion points. However, in Chapter Three we showed that black officers are substantially less likely to separate during "retention periods," when their separation decision would be voluntary.

There is little broader evidence to support a contention that black officers believe that they have greater civilian job opportunities than do their white counterparts. Data from the 1992 SOEP show few differences in civilian opportunities, career intentions, or satisfaction with military life between black and white officers (of either gender). Black officers are actually less likely than are white officers of the same gender to have received a job offer from a civilian employer and no more likely to have actively looked for work in the past year (see Figure 10).[22] Similarly, black officers are no more likely than

---

[22]The tabulations in Figures 10 and 11 are for officers in grades O-1 through O-4 only. The statistical significances of the racial differences between males and between females for receipt of job offers (Figure 10) and having actively looked for a civilian job (Figure 10) were evaluated by using a logistic regression where the regressors were dichotomous variables for race, for gender, and for a race/gender interaction. The statistical significances of the racial differences for the chances of finding a good civilian job (Figure 10) were evaluated by using both an ordinary least squares regression and an ordered logistic regression on the 11-point scale given to respondents with similar regressors as before. The statistical significances of the racial differences for the ex-

are white officers to believe that they could easily find a good civilian job (see Figure 10).[23] There are no substantive differences between black and white officers in the year of service at which they expect to separate (see Figure 10) or in satisfaction with the general way of life in the military (see Figure 11).

BIAS IN FAVOR OF BLACKS

White male officers believed that any bias that exists in the system is against themselves rather than against blacks or women. One white participant stated: "If a minority has everything, is qualified for something, but has lower test scores than a white with all the right qualifications, the minority will get it." A few white officers stated that they understood that boards are given either explicit orders or heavy pressure to promote blacks and women at rates equal to white men, regardless of their career record. One white officer stated, "I think some officers get promoted because they are female, because they are black. . . . I don't know how they promote people in D.C., but I know they have quotas. I have seen too many incompetent minorities." Another stated:

> This is the rumor, that the board was given a letter of instruction that said "when you read a woman's or minority's OPR,[24] you must assume that they were discriminated against, so you must score them higher than you do the others."

---

pected years of completed service (Figure 10) were evaluated by using both ordinary least squares regression on actual expected years of completed service and by logistic regression on whether the respondent expected to complete 20 or more years of service with similar regressors as before. The statistical significances of the racial differences for the satisfaction with military life (Figure 11), satisfaction with coworkers (Figure 11), support from supervisors (Figure 11), and effect of current assignment on promotion chances (Figure 11) were evaluated by using an ordered logistic regression on the 5-point scales given to respondents with similar regressors as before.

[23]There are no statistically significant differences between black and white men or between black and white women in their reported chances of having received a civilian job offer, their reported chances of having looked for a civilian job in the past year, their perception of their civilian job opportunities, the number of years they expect to serve, or their satisfaction with the military way of life.

[24]Officer Performance Report.

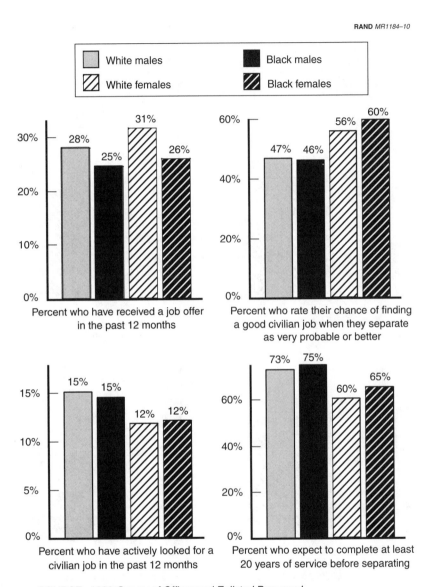

SOURCE: 1992 *Survey of Officer and Enlisted Personnel.*

Figure 10—Civilian Job Expectations of O-1–O-4 Officers

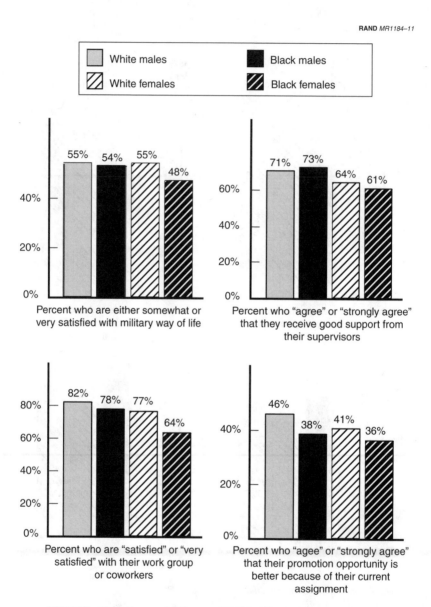

RAND *MR1184–11*

SOURCE: 1992 *Survey of Officer and Enlisted Personnel.*

Figure 11—Satisfaction of O-1–O-4 Officers with Career Attributes

This perception also runs counter to the data we reported in Chapter Three on the relative diminished promotion chances of black officers. Yet since board results are not published in an aggregated format by race or gender, officers generally have little information by which to confirm or reject their beliefs about the board outcomes for blacks and women.[25]

Many white midcareer officers misunderstood the precepts that govern the deliberations of promotion boards. As we described in Chapter Two, at the time of our fieldwork, the precepts stated as a goal rather than a requirement the promotion of women and minorities at rates equivalent to white males. The services had procedures for tracking how well the goals were being met during the board's proceedings, although in some cases the procedures were carried out only if requested by the board president. At the conclusion of all boards, the results were tallied to assess how well the board had met the precept goals. A board could be asked to reconsider its decision if the outcome was substantially out of balance with the goals; yet the board members we talked to reported that reconsideration rarely occurred.

In some services, the precepts instructed board members to be aware that discrimination may have disadvantaged minorities and women during their careers. Board members reported that this instruction

---

[25]The perceptions of the precepts regarding women and minorities among white officers in our discussions were consistent with the range of more general societal attitudes regarding affirmative action programs. Support of affirmative action programs among whites has been found to vary considerably under a variety of scenarios. Support decreases when programs run counter to an individual's immediate self-interest (Bobo and Kluegel, 1993; Kluegel and Smith, 1983; Nosworthy et al., 1995). The military's up-or-out promotion system combined with force downsizing has created the widespread perception of a zero-sum environment for advancement. As a result, white officers may see personnel policies that focus special attention on minorities as increasingly running counter to their own self-interest.

On the other hand, support increases when programs are seen as limited to increasing equality of opportunity. Programs focused on recruiting or initial training receive more support than programs that treat minorities differently once they are incorporated into an organization (Kravitz, 1995; Kravitz and Platania, 1993; Nosworthy, et al., 1995; Steeh and Krysan, 1996). Correspondingly, support for programs is weak among those who view the stratification system of an organization, or society, as already basically egalitarian (Kluegel and Smith, 1982). To the extent that an officer perceives that career success is driven solely by performance, he or she may be less likely to support personnel policies that treat minorities differently.

sometimes helps them to understand an anomalous negative performance report in an otherwise consistent record of strong performance reports. However, the board members we interviewed generally felt that, except in the most obvious cases, it is quite difficult to distinguish subtle discrimination against an officer from average or weak performance by the officer. As one board member stated,

> You could be very sensitive to [race and gender] issues after the [board's instructional] briefing, but when you get ready to raise your hand, you cannot say whether a minority officer has a poor file because he is a poor performer, or because he was victimized. The training you get gives you some understanding of how these people were disadvantaged, but it still would not help because it was too late.

Further, board members generally felt that the board process is not the place to make corrections for past injustices. A board member observed,

> If there is a weakness, it is in the information you are given. If OERs[26] do not accurately reflect performance, or if a person never had the opportunity to serve in good jobs, then the board cannot compensate for that, and should not.

Nearly all officers interviewed who had been involved with a board proceeding expressed a belief that the boards do the best job possible given the materials that are before them. They believed that if members of a group tended to have less success in the board process, it came from the quality of the files presented to the board rather than from differential treatment by the board.

Most board members in our discussions felt that if all indications of race and gender were removed from the file, little change would occur in the board outcomes. A recent analysis of Navy and Marine Corps promotion board results by Mehay (1995) provides some factual basis for this perception. Mehay has found that Navy and Marine Corps O-4 promotion board decisions closely reflect the performance evaluations that officers receive, regardless of race. In

---

[26]Officer Evaluation Reports.

addition, some board members felt that removing race and gender identifiers from the file might hurt the promotion chances of women and minorities because they would have no context for understanding particularly anomalous performance reports. Many minority and women officers agreed. The consensus was that, except in the most obvious cases, it was quite difficult to distinguish subtle discrimination against an officer from average or weak performance by the officer. Further, officers who had served as board members generally felt that, since there is an appeals process for performance evaluations, the promotion board is not the place to make corrections for past injustices.

Most black officers whom we interviewed readily recognized that some white officers perceive board precepts to favor minorities and women, but they scoffed at the notion that they receive an advantage in the career-management system. Some black officers expressed concern that such policies reinforce the stereotypes that blacks are less capable and do not succeed on their own merit. There is concern among some that these policies give little benefit to minorities yet provide military leadership with a claim to have adequately addressed racial inequities. While many black officers expressed some sympathy with this argument, few advocated removing the relevant statements from board precepts.

To be clear, no black officer was interested in receiving a promotion or assignment that he or she did not deserve or was not fully qualified for. As one black officer commented, "Personally, I would hate to get a billet because of affirmative action—I would feel less qualified than the next guy." The precepts are not seen as providing an advantage, just as "a check to make sure that everyone is playing honest."

SUMMARY

A common perception among white officers for why fewer black officers attain senior ranks is that more black officers choose to separate to pursue civilian employment opportunities. We found no evidence to support this common perception. In fact, black officers appear more likely to choose to remain in the service. Instead, our data analysis showed that the key to understanding racial differences in career development appears to be the lower probability that black officers receive promotions.

Midcareer officers, regardless of race, believed that promotion boards are fair in their deliberations, and the available evidence supports this view. The more limited career progression of black officers appears to be due to difficulty in compiling competitive performance records. On the basis of both our research and the research of others, we believe that the most likely causes of this difficulty are weaker precommissioning preparation and more limited social integration.

The structure of our study did not allow us to directly evaluate the precommissioning preparation of black officers. Officers told us that an officer can overcome a slow start, but this must happen early in his or her career. Other research, although limited, does find that, on average, white officers enter with more competitive educational backgrounds than black officers. However, the differences in precommissioning preparation were insufficient, in and of themselves, to explain the racial differences in promotion chances.

Our discussions with both white and black officers suggest that a key problem for black officers is their greater difficulty forming peer and mentor relationships. White and black officers both discussed how such relationships provide important resources for succeeding at one's current assignment as well as for opening future career opportunities. We could not objectively measure differences in the ability to form and draw from peer and mentor relationships, yet comments from both white and black officers made it clear that a certain level of social segregation continues to exist between the two groups.

The limited access to peer and mentor networks and limited precommissioning preparation described by focus group participants may lessen the chances, on average, that black officers get selected for career-enhancing assignments and duties. Disproportionate assignment of minorities to duties outside their occupations may further disadvantage black officers by placing them in assignments that are generally seen as less career enhancing. The final result appears to be that black officers, as a group, bring somewhat less competitive career records before promotion boards.

The degree to which this stems from limited opportunities to demonstrate their skills and abilities or weaker precommissioning preparation is worthy of further consideration.

Chapter Five

OFFICERS' PERCEPTIONS OF GENDER DIFFERENCES IN CAREER PROGRESSION

In Chapter Three, we documented that women are more likely to leave during retention periods, where separation decisions are most likely to be voluntary. This result is supported by survey data showing that junior women are less likely to anticipate a full 20-year career (Figure 10). In this chapter we present the common perceptions offered by officers as to why career progression differs for women and men. We draw here on the same focus groups and one-on-one interviews with officers described in Chapter Four to explore why such gender differences exist.

Unless otherwise stated, the issues discussed in this chapter apply equally to both black women and white women. As we noted in the last chapter, black women did not raise any issues in our discussion that were also not discussed by either black men or white women. Similarly, unless otherwise stated, those perceptions we represent as "male" are held by both black and white men, and those perceptions represented as "female" are held by both black and white women. Our conversations with black men focused primarily on racial issues; as a consequence, some gender issues were discussed with white men but not black men. Where we had little basis to assert that black men concurred or disagreed with comments by white men, we have attributed the perspective only to white men. Therefore, care must be taken not to assume that black men disagreed with perspectives attributed to white men.

Perceptions represent how members of each group interpret their experiences in the career-management system; they are important and telling in and of themselves. As we will discuss, men and women often offer distinct and contradictory explanations for group differences in career progress. Yet as we cautioned in the prior chapter, an individual's perception of an interaction can be inaccurate if he or she misjudges the motives or assumptions of others. Thus, its meaning needs to be evaluated against broader information about group differences in career experiences. After we present the common explanations offered by each group, we also discuss other evidence from our research and the research of others that supports or refutes these perceptions.

WHY DO WOMEN CHOOSE TO LEAVE?

Most officers, men and women, recognized that the services have room for improvement in dealing with gender issues. Most men in our discussions readily expected the career progress of women to be more limited than that of men. While an end goal of equality of opportunity and treatment was taken as a given in the context of race and ethnicity, in our discussions with midcareer officers, there was no consensus on appropriate military roles for women. Not only did men and women disagree on this issue, there was also a diversity of opinion within gender groups about the appropriate military role for women.

Male officers in our discussions offered various reasons why they expected differences in the career development of men and women. They mentioned three primary reasons:

- Women are inherently less capable, physically and mentally, to perform a military job and lead troops.

- Past and ongoing prohibitions on assigning women to combat occupations have kept them out of occupations with the greatest career opportunities.

- The fear among male superiors of finding themselves in a position from which they could not refute an unwarranted charge of sexual harassment interferes with important interactions between male superior officers and their female subordinates.

The first assertion follows the same general theme expressed by whites about minorities and the racial differences in career progression: women do not have the necessary skills and abilities to make senior ranks. The last assertion, that fear of being charged with sexual harassment interferes with important interactions between men and women, was unique in that a broad group of officers admitted to treating the members of another group differently.

Additionally, as in the discussions regarding racial bias in the career-management system, some white men went a step further and expressed the belief that women are advantaged by the career-management system. Similar to those who perceive an advantage for minorities in the career-management system, officers offered the promotion goals of board precepts and other personnel policies that explicitly treat women differently as proof of this advantage. We address this issue of bias in favor of women near the end of this chapter, but we first wish to fully explore the issues related to bias against women.

Like male officers, women by and large agreed with the premise that performance is the major determinant of an officer's success; yet they also believed that factors other than one's skills and abilities influence an officer's performance. Similar to blacks, women perceived that their opportunities to perform and the recognition they receive are diminished by expectations that they are less capable, have difficulties forming peer and mentor relationships, and receive fewer career-enhancing assignments. Women also expressed several additional reasons for difficulties in their career development:

- Sexual harassment creates an uncomfortable working environment for women who are harassed.

- Male officers' fears of being charged with sexual harassment have placed a pall on the interactions between men and women.

- The demands of assignments often come into conflict with family responsibilities, sometimes unnecessarily.

- There continues to be no clear consensus among military personnel on the appropriate role for women in the military.

Given the difficulties that women felt they regularly faced and given their sense of a lack of clear roles for women in the institution, a disproportionate number of women officers may be concluding that it is not worthwhile to continue to invest in a military career.

Thus, our separate discussions with men and women raised a common set of issues to explain differences in career experiences: inherent skills and abilities, assignment patterns and available career paths, sexual harassment and social integration, and competing opportunities and obligations. While this set of issues resembles those raised to explain racial differences, the nature of how each issue plays out is sometimes quite different.

INHERENT SKILLS AND ABILITIES

There are a wide variety of occupations and duties in the military. Many are no different from civilian jobs, and some are similar to occupations traditionally dominated by women. However, combat and combat-related occupations and duties traditionally have been viewed as a male domain, with women restricted from serving in all such occupations or duties until quite recently. One assumption made by many men and some women is that women do not have the physical or emotional character to handle the stresses of combat. One male officer offered a particularly colorful observation:

> Anyone can do a staff job if you keep your sanity long enough. There's little difference in men and women on these jobs. Combat jobs are different. I know of a woman who got her fingernail caught in an M16 rifle and threw the gun down and swore about breaking a nail. Men wouldn't do that. . . . When it came time for low crawls, there was a reticence among the women to do that.

Most men in our discussions readily offered and accepted the contention that women have weaker physical capabilities, so discussions quickly moved toward other aspects such as leadership capabilities. Leadership is considered a particularly important skill for an officer. Men and women told us that the military has tended to favor a physical, aggressive leadership style. "Leadership is equated with aggressive. Supervisors tend to like aggressive leadership styles," observed a male officer. Some men acknowledged that they find it hard to view women as strong leaders because of the inherent difficulty they believe women have projecting this leadership style.[1] One male

---

[1]In civilian settings, where physical capabilities are less of an issue, studies have demonstrated that women are generally less likely to be viewed as capable managers

board member noted, "There are women that have believability, credibility, and are feminine, but can she really go ahead and be a leader? Will she really be accepted into all levels?" Another commented:

> We tend to use ourselves as a yardstick by which we measure others. Women have different leadership styles. . . . There are so many men in leadership, so we tend to favor male styles. We have no preparation for doing anything different, because we don't have that many females as colleagues or as superiors.

Most women recognized that men view them as inherently less capable. Asked if her gender mattered in how she was treated, one woman responded:

> It matters—yes! Gender—very much so, and no doubt I'm not respected as much as males—I'm not a warrior—that stinks. Stereotypes are still in place—subtle but still there. I don't like that very much. You still have to prove yourself—this summarizes the whole gender problem.

The sense that "you have to prove yourself" was often expressed in our discussions. One woman commented, "For a guy, it is assumed you will be a success until it is proven otherwise, but for a woman, it is assumed that you will be a failure until proven otherwise." Another commented, "A boss who is not familiar with working with women will always test [a new female subordinate]."

The women in the focus groups agreed that questions of women's qualifications often surrounded their physical skills and capabilities. In some units, members perform physical training (PT) exercises together at some point in the day. Several women perceived that their superior officers used this as an opportunity to explicitly test their physical capabilities, a test they asserted is generally not given to new male subordinates.[2] One woman relayed the following experience:

---

or leaders (Martin et al., 1983; Schein, 1978; Steckler and Rosenthal, 1985). As for minorities, women find it more difficult to establish their ability (Biernat and Kobrynowicz, 1997).

[2]None of the men we talked with suggested that they had been tested in this manner.

> I showed up for PT the first morning with a terrible head cold. I was dying out there, but the last thing I would do is admit it. I held on. There were men falling out behind me, but I was still there. Finally, some of the guys said to the commander, "Why are we running so far? We never go this far." Everyone else shut them up. They didn't want me to know they had raised the standard to see if they could eliminate me.

After relaying a similar story, another woman commented: "My credibility was judged on that first day based on my physical prowess, not my intelligence, which is what I really needed to do that job."

The women who related such experiences were clearly bothered that they had been subjected to a test that others had not. "I'll achieve any standard that is set . . . but don't evaluate me on a standard that isn't there," one said. Yet many of these women found that after successfully passing the test, they were then treated quite well by their commanding officer. Another woman who successfully passed such a test found that "after that, I could do no wrong in that . . . brigade."

Personal experiences of such explicit tests were offered by a relatively small number of women. All were officers in either the Army or the Marine Corps. However, most women, regardless of service, expressed that at some time they had found it necessary to "educate" new coworkers, subordinates, or commanders that working with women need not be any different than working with men. One woman reported the following experience:

> One guy told me he has no use for women. But after we went through CAS3[3] together, he came up to me and said, "You taught me that women do have a role in the Army." Men need to work with women in order to be able to judge them and accept them.

Many of the men we interviewed have had female peers or subordinates, but it should be noted that few had ever served under a female commanding officer. Those who had served under a woman gener-

---

[3]Combined Arms and Service Staff School.

ally spoke well of their experience, but many male officers seemed to prefer to have a male superior.[4]

For this study we had no means for evaluating actual differences in the skills and abilities of women, yet other research contains little evidence for the contention that women are rated as less capable. Mehay (1995) has found that Navy women officers have been more likely than men to receive recommendations for early promotion on their fitness report (FITREPs). Cymrot and Lawler (1990) have found that women are more likely than their male peers on similar types of ships to attain the Navy's Surface Warfare Officer (SWO) qualification.[5] Augmentation and promotion board outcomes also provide little support for the argument that women officers are less qualified. Our quantitative analysis of women officers in all four services found that women did not have lower chances than men of being promoted, controlling for race. Studies of officer promotion in the Navy and Marine Corps (North et al., 1995, and Mehay, 1995) have found that women were promoted at higher rates than were men.

Finally, one study of Marine women officers contradicts the perception that women are evaluated as less capable leaders. North et al. (1995) have examined the relationship between augmentation, promotion and voluntary separation, and the three skill rankings (leadership, academic, and military) received by officer candidates during TBS between 1985 and 1987. Of the three skill rankings, leadership has the strongest positive relationship with augmentation and promotion chances, and the strongest negative relationship to voluntary separations. Women had nearly equivalent leadership skill rankings as did their male peers. However, women did score slightly lower on academic skill rankings and meaningfully lower on military skill rankings.

---

[4]The preference for a male superior has been found in some settings among both male and female civilian employees as well (Hansen, 1974; Haccoun et al., 1978; Kanter et al., 1977), yet is absent in others (Rosen and Jerdee, 1973; Bartol, 1975). In a study of semiskilled workers, Trempe et al. (1985) find that the preference for a male supervisor derives primarily from a perception that the supervisor's gender is seen as a proxy for upward organizational influence.

[5]Until recently, women have only been able to serve as SWO-qualified officers in the combat logistics force (CLF) or on ships other than aircraft carriers, cruisers, or destroyers. Of the women pursuing SWO qualification, 98 percent were serving on one of these other types of ships and 2 percent were in the CLF.

ASSIGNMENT PATTERNS AND AVAILABLE CAREER PATHS

Chapter Two summarized the recent changes in the occupational and assignment restrictions for women. These changes were in an early stage of implementation when we held the focus groups and discussions for this project. However, the attitudes of participants in this study toward combat roles for women are consistent with the attitudes of participants in a recent study of units and occupations that were opened to women by recent policy changes (Harrell and Miller, 1997).

Shifts in societal attitudes have certainly been among the drivers of the recent opening of most occupations and duties previously closed to women; our discussions revealed a lack of consensus for allowing women to serve in combat roles. Most men we talked to still believed that combat remains an inappropriate role for women. These discussions did not distinguish between ground combat and other forms of combat, as current policy does. Participants in our discussions justified the restrictions of women from certain occupations and assignments with a concern over women's abilities and a lack of "social legitimacy" for the role of women in combat. Male officers in our discussions generally found it difficult to distinguish between these two issues. One male officer simply stated, "Women can't and shouldn't serve in combat positions." Another commented, "There is no one in combat arms who really thinks women should be in that MOS [Military Occupational Specialty]. Women can never overcome the stigma of being lesser [officers] because the organization endorses that."

The justifications expressed for restrictions regarding ground combat were not solely based on societal attitudes or the capabilities of women, but also on the effect of women on the men in a combat unit. One male commented, "Unit bonding may be disrupted because some people want to date [women]. I've seen some pretty immature jealousies arise in these situations. It interferes with the combat environment." A female officer offered the experience that during a "meeting of our leadership group . . . one guy came out and said that women degrade the war-fighting spirit."

Some men and most women expressed a belief that women who meet uniform performance standards should be free to pursue any military occupational specialty or duty assignment that they wish. One officer stated:

> I don't personally care if women are in combat arms, as long as they meet the same standards as men. I expect women to be in combat arms in the future. If the women cannot meet the same physical standards, it will ruin their reputation. A woman cannot fall out on a really hard hike or the respect of their fellow officers and those under their command will collapse. This is true for all officers, not just those in combat arms.

Women also wanted to ensure that the physical standards set for a particular job be truly in line with the demands of that job. Currently, the services can assign men to combat occupations, regardless of their preferences, according to the services' needs. Women, however, are not assigned to combat occupations against their wishes.[6] Some of the women but few of the men we interviewed felt that both sexes should be treated equally for combat assignments, conditional on service members meeting a uniform physical standard.[7]

The opinions expressed in our interviews are generally consistent with the findings of Harrell and Miller (1997). In their survey, 63 percent of the male officers were satisfied with the present regulations restricting women from ground combat, 14 percent felt that women should be able to volunteer for the restricted occupations and unit assignments, and 22 percent felt that women and men should be treated the same. Among women officers in the survey, 41 percent felt that women should be treated the same as men and another 41 percent felt that women should be able to volunteer for ground combat.

Many officers saw the past and remaining restrictions on combat-related assignments as a significant limiting factor for a woman's military career. "If you don't put fire and iron on a target, you're a

---

[6]Women are currently permitted in most non-ground combat-related occupations.

[7]GAO (1998) points out that different standards are allowed for general fitness, but not allowed by law for job qualification. The report further concludes that general fitness standards are not scientifically based. Thus, perceptions about the relative difficulty of the male and female standards cannot be evaluated.

second-class officer (or lower)," explained one officer. Another explained that "as they rise higher in the organization, women don't command the same confidence that they can lead at the highest ranks as men, because they don't come from the combat arms branch." Regardless of occupational specialty, some women offered a broader concern that restrictions on their assignments have reinforced a view that women are not the equals of men as military officers. One senior woman officer commented:

> There is a climate created when you say you cannot do something because of your gender. By your description you are not up for those things. In my heart of hearts I do not think women should be in the infantry. But I would never say that publicly, because I remember how discouraging that is.

Most men and women we interviewed saw the restrictions on women from holding certain occupations and assignments within occupations as an important factor inhibiting the potential advancement of women. Successful command experience was considered important for advancement to senior ranks. Most officers expected that individuals in noncombat occupations, regardless of gender, have more restricted opportunities to advance beyond O-4 because of the limited command opportunities in the support occupations. Thus, both male and female officers believed that one reason women are less likely to stay is the perception of more limited opportunities in noncombat occupations.

The women we interviewed initiated their careers when many more military occupations and assignments were closed to women. This has made it difficult for women in some occupations, particularly those related to combat, to plan appropriate career moves, as they sometimes found that the logical next career move was not open to them. As one woman commented, "You just aren't sure of the progression track now." Another offered, "There is no real defined career path for me—so it's like looking at a list of 80 or so people in my field and saying 'What can I shoot for next?'" This has also made it difficult for the commanders of some women to offer appropriate career advice.

Many women officers cited shifts in the implementation of policy in questioning the long-term opportunities for fully advancing their careers. One woman officer perceived changing practices regarding women in artillery positions:

> It seemed for a while there that one year women were in, then they weren't the next year, then they were in the year later. It constantly flip-flopped. So women were in a position there of saying, "Now I have a career, now I don't have a career." A lot of them were forced out by all of this back and forth. They got out because they knew they would hit a ceiling based on the fact that they hadn't consistently had the opportunity to perform within the branch and because of all of the uncertainty regarding their status within the branch.

Many women officers questioned whether their service is committed to providing them with full career opportunities and cited this as a reason to separate for alternative opportunities.

Little data are available for testing the perception that differences in promotion and retention between men and women are related to occupation, assignment practices, or selection for professional military education (GAO, 1998). As we reported in Chapter Three, the concentration of women in noncombat occupations explains only a small amount of the greater chances of separation that women experience. Thus, our analyses indicates that the concentration of women in support occupations does not offer a compelling explanation for the scarcity of women in the senior ranks.

SEXUAL HARASSMENT AND SOCIAL INTEGRATION

Our discussions regarding the social integration and acceptance of women generally centered on the issues of harassment and the current environment deriving from the services' efforts to address harassment. Women reported that sexual harassment occurs and is often difficult to confront or report. The experiences and perceptions regarding sexual harassment raised by women in our conversa- 'tions are broadly consistent with the findings of several other studies and surveys of military women.[8] By and large, men dismissed the reported relative frequency of harassment incidents. Many men in

---

[8]In particular, see GAO (1996), Harrell and Miller (1997), and Bastian et al. (1996).

our conversations felt that incidents are often attributable to misunderstandings. Some men saw women as being too quick to ascribe the cause for any confrontation to gender discrimination or harassment.[9]

An important dimension of the problem that has often been overlooked in other studies is the effect that the current environment has on relationships beyond those immediately involved in harassment situations. Many men believe that the institution has become overreactive to accusations of harassment. As a result, these men try to avoid situations where their intentions or motivations might be misinterpreted. The women in our conversations were quite cognizant that some men hold this belief. Most women and men were concerned about the cost of this behavior to women peers and subordinates. This behavior is certain to inhibit women officers' ability to draw support and assistance from peer and mentor relationships. Worse, it may close off key career-enhancing assignments for women when such an assignment would require a close working relationship with a male officer.

Harassment[10]

We did not include specific questions about sexual harassment in our interview protocols. Instead, we allowed participants to raise the issue as they deemed appropriate in the context of our broader discussion of problems related to career progression.[11]

Women raised the issue of sexual harassment in every focus group we conducted. Many women reported that they had been harassed at some point in their career and that they believe harassment con-

---

[9]The more explicit that the social-sexual behavior is in a situation, the greater the agreement between men and women on the offensiveness of the situation and the certainty that harassment occurred. In situations with greater ambiguity, women have been found to be more likely to perceive a situation as harassment than have men (Frazier et al., 1995; Williams et al., 1995).

[10]Other recent studies on this issue include GAO (1995, 1996), Bastian et al. (1996), Culbertson et al. (1993), Air Force Inspector General (1993), Firestone and Harris (1994), and The Secretary of the Army (1997).

[11]It should be noted that our discussions occurred before the reports of harassment at Army training facilities surfaced, but after the Tailhook incident, during which Navy female officers were harassed at an annual convention of aviators.

tinues to occur with some frequency. The situations related to us included efforts to undermine or sabotage a woman's work, demeaning or inappropriate comments, inappropriate and persistent unwanted sexual advances, and physical sexual attacks by another service member.[12]

Most of the harassment situations discussed occurred at an earlier time in the officer's career, yet some were more recent. In and of itself, this should not be taken as a sign that the frequency of harassment has declined; junior officers may simply be more likely to be victims of harassment.[13] The 1995 Department of Defense Sexual Harassment Survey has documented a substantial decline in the proportion of women who report having been harassed in the past year (Bastian et al., 1996). However, despite the decline, more than half of female service members continue to report having been subjected to unwanted sexual attention in the past year.

In our focus groups, women reported that their options for recourse are seen as fraught with dangers to their own careers. In general, they felt that officers are supposed to be able to take care of problems on their own. Women who complain to their commanders are seen as risking being viewed as weak. Said one woman:

> When the [offender] is of the same rank, you want to deal with them on your own. If you go to your chain of command, they say it is because you are a woman, you can't hold your own and you need to run and cry to someone.

This woman pointed to a second danger in complaining about harassment: being seen as betraying your peers, undermining the cohesion of your unit, or being viewed as having an independent agenda. One woman commented:

---

[12]See Miller (1997) for an important discussion on the distinction between sexual and gender harassment.

[13]Bastian et al. (1996) have reported that junior enlisted women are more likely than senior enlisted women to be subjected to a harassment incident. Their results for officers are not broken out by junior and senior status. Yet it is reasonable to assume that a similar relationship might hold for officers.

Sometimes people, in this case women, feel like they are holding a "This is offensive to me" card and abuse it because it gives them more power.

Another woman commented:

I chose to let things go because I thought I would suffer more than he would. . . . They would mark me down on loyalty, [that's] the "velvet hammer."

The danger of being seen as betraying one's unit or having an independent agenda is thought to be particularly high if a woman submits a formal complaint that might lead to an outside investigation. One woman concluded that "even now [efforts to deal with] sexual harassment are a joke, because I have seen people's careers ruined if they reported problems."[14]

Women reported a number of mechanisms to cope with sexual harassment. The most common approach appeared to be to tolerate the situation and look for a way out. For lesser problems like inappropriate verbal comments, many women employed humor to defuse the situation. One woman told a particularly colorful story:

I really think that one of the most essential tools a junior officer has to develop is comebacks . . . that can be pulled out that allow you to deal with them in a humorous but effective way. I [was to provide] counseling to this platoon sergeant. . . . I get to his tent and tell the private there who I'm looking for and he goes in. Then I hear him say "Tell the [female-specific expletive] I'll be with her in a minute." . . . We spent three hours talking about it and finally worked it all out . . . Looking back on it now, I know just how I would have handled it. When he came out I just would have said, "That's Major [female-specific expletive] to you." . . . If I had had that comeback, I think the whole thing would have been nipped in the bud.

_____

[14]A recent GAO study of the services' sexual harassment complaint systems also found that enlisted and junior officer women feared reprisals for filing an EO complaint or doubted that a complaint would be acted on by the chain of command (1996). The 1995 DoD Sexual Harassment Survey found that about 20 percent of women service members did not feel free to report an incidence of sexual harassment without fear of "bad things happening," and another 30 percent felt some limited concern about reporting sexual harassment (Bastian et al., 1996).

In addition, some women expressed concern about filing a formal complaint. There was a perspective, among both men and women, that when complaints are acted on, they can end the offending officer's career. For minor transgressions, some women felt this to be an extreme punishment. Thus, they chose to simply suffer the indignity rather than report it, as they did not believe the offense to be significant enough for the possible punishment.[15] Some women felt that for many situations, the best approach to dealing with incidents was to directly confront the offender. As one woman commented: "It is really incumbent on you to say something. If it is happening to you, it is happening to soldiers who don't have the ability you have to do something about it." Others disagreed:

> I would emphasize the importance of not playing the gender card. Being in that minority, you don't think you are playing that card and you may not be. But the perception out there is that you are.

A few women found that their male peers will confront those who make inappropriate comments. One officer related her experience:

> We all had our PT test. I maxed my test, my [boss] failed his. I was the only female in the group that took it. There were a group of officers who failed their test hanging around waiting to get chewed out. I come in and he looks at me and says, "Lieutenant, how did you do? "I maxed!" So he says, "Oh, I heard only dykes max the test." I went back to him later and said that if you need help, I'll give it to you, but your comment was inappropriate. He apologized and said that others had chewed him out for it after I had walked away. I really think that confronting this is important.

Another related a discussion of war-fighting spirit:

---

[15]Research on sexual harassment in civilian and military employment has found that the majority of incidents go unreported. The 1995 DoD Sexual Harassment Survey found that only about one-quarter of those experiencing a harassing incident reported their experience (Bastian et al., 1996). Common reasons given by victims to explain why they did not report their situation are that they took care of it themselves, feared retaliation or humiliation, believed that nothing could or would get done, or desired not to cause problems for the harasser (Fitzgerald et al., 1995, Gutek and Koss, 1993; Martindale, 1990; Bastian et al., 1996; GAO, 1996; Harrell and Miller, 1997). Instead, victims reported relying primarily on either avoidance or appeasement of harassers to put them off without direct confrontation (Fitzgerald et al., 1995).

> One guy came out and said that women degrade the war-fighting spirit. . . . I'm in a good group. The guy next to me took this guy on. He started talking about how women bring certain kinds of skills, increase the talent pool, comments like that.

Yet few women reported such supportive behavior by their male peers.

Men's Hesitancy in Interactions with Women

Men expressed a very clear sense that the current environment surrounding the enforcement of sexual harassment charges casts a pall on the appropriate and necessary interactions between men and women.[16] It was common for men to believe that a charge of sexual harassment, even if ultimately unproven, could end an officer's career. Women readily recognized the prevalence of this perception among men, even though many women believed that their command would take little action against someone accused of sexual harassment. Given these high stakes, some men expressed that they have limited or controlled their interactions with women in order to reduce the chances that a harassment charge could be raised.

In its most benign form, the problem dampens social interactions. One male officer commented:

> I am guarded right now, because I am worried about saying the wrong thing; whereas before I could make some innocent comments. It's a killjoy, and camaraderie is reduced. It puts a damper on social interactions with women.

Many women saw this inhibition as increasing the already present barriers to their social acceptance. One woman commented, "The men are scared to death of it. Now they are afraid to have fun." Yet men and women saw the problem as going considerably further, interfering with the ability to provide necessary performance feedback to women.

---

[16] The hesitation that men feel in their working relationships with women colleagues that we report here is strikingly similar to that reported by Harrell and Miller (1997).

Less benign are the inhibitions male commanders reported in their interactions with subordinate female officers. One male officer commented, "People worry about confronting someone and being hit with a sexual harassment charge. . . . How do you deal with sub-par women without losing face when you're afraid of confronting them?" Another male officer offered the following comment on the current situation:

> Enough [men] are so concerned that the allegation [of sexual ha-rassment] is so bad, that one should go out of their way to avoid being accused. If you're not there, you're less likely to be accused, but you're also less likely to mentor. You are not going to sit in a room mentoring a female, or if you do you are going to make sure that the door is open. You're sure as hell not going to get in a HUMV and say, "Let's go talk about the situation."

In a similar vein, a woman commented, "The fear is there . . . that if they correct females on a professional issue, like the uniform, they will be accused [of sexual harassment]."

This problem may particularly hurt outstanding women, as senior male officers may be more hesitant to select women for key assistant positions in which the senior officer would have substantial private interaction. One senior male officer commented:

> You can't pay too much attention to female officers because of sex-ual harassment. For instance, if you select an Aide de Camp, you can select any male you want. But if you select a female, that will generate talk. So a lot of male officers will not select women for that job.

The services' efforts to educate and sensitize officers to what consti-tutes sexual harassment were seen by some women as problematic in and of themselves. Stated one woman:

> The whole Tailhook thing, for instance, that really spun me. It was sexual assault pure and simple and it should have dealt with that head-on. Instead we got a "stand-down." The mandatory training was sophomoric and simplistic. The whole male Navy walked away from the training with the wrong idea. The Navy went overboard.

Some women saw *any* policies that draw distinctions between men and women as causing more harm than good. One woman commented, "We should really avoid policies that select out based on sex. This is what leads to craziness." Another commented, "Stop making gender an issue. By not talking and focusing on it, they will look at me as a naval officer only."

COMPETING OPPORTUNITIES AND OBLIGATIONS

Next to the issue of sexual harassment and the environment that the management of it is currently creating, the conflicts between being an officer and caring for your family were the most talked-about topics in our discussions. Women officers make decisions regarding work and family in a substantially different context than do men. The marital status of officers provides a relatively stark illustration of this different context. The overwhelming norm for field-grade male officers is to be married and to have a spouse who is not in the military (see Figure 12). In contrast, only slightly more than half of all field-grade women officers are married. Among men at O-4 or at a higher rank, 79 percent are married and only 3 percent have a spouse who is on active duty; while among women at the same ranks, only 45 percent are married and 28 percent have a spouse on active duty. Focusing on officers with young children at home, Figure 13 shows that far more women are single parents or have working spouses. Thus, women officers are facing different constraints than their male counterparts in their efforts to mix work and family.

Many women said that they had expected certain conflicts between the life of an officer and the responsibilities of caring for a family. Yet even though many of these women were willing to put, as one woman said, "service above self," they saw conflicts as arising unnecessarily, deriving more from an adherence to tradition than from a requirement for completing one's assignment. Women spoke most about two particular problem areas: child-care arrangements and military spouse considerations.

The difficulties associated with separations from family, managing two careers, and child-care arrangements are not unique to women officers. The toll of military life on one's spouse or family was a reason expressed by many men for why they would consider separating from the military. Some men also commented on difficulties juggling

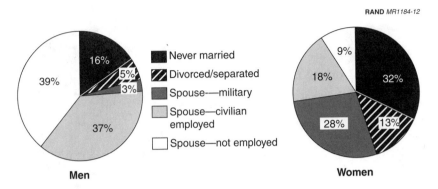

RAND *MR1184-12*

SOURCE: 1992 *Survey of Officer and Enlisted Personnel.*

Figure 12—Marital Status of Men and Women at the Rank of O-4 or Higher

their work schedule and child-care arrangements. Yet the careers of women officers are disproportionately affected by these problems because of the greater likelihood that they are married to a working spouse or are raising children on their own.[17]

Child-Care Arrangements

Every focus group with women officers turned at some point to the difficulties caused by insufficient availability of child care. Women officers are more likely than men to rely on day care for their children. In addition, women officers with children are more likely than their male peers with children to be either unmarried or in a dual-working couple (see Figure 13). Military officers are often expected to work long and atypical hours. Such a work schedule can be incompatible with the rules and regulations of both military and

[17]Difficulties combining career and family are not unique to military women; women in the civilian labor force also face considerable difficulties. Goldin (1995) studied the patterns of career employment, marriage, and childbearing among a nationally representative sample of married women who were ages 37–47 in 1991. Of these women less than one-fifth were both a parent and employed in career-oriented work.

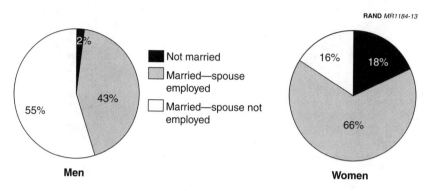

SOURCE: 1992 *Survey of Officer and Enlisted Personnel.*

**Figure 13—Spouse's Employment Status of Officers with
Children Age Six or Younger**

civilian day care establishments. Laws and day care agency policies often limit the total time that children can spend in day care, and many child-care centers, military and civilian, levy steep fines for picking up one's child after a designated closing time.

Many women officers found it hard to understand why the services could not ensure the availability of child care for the hours that they are required to work. For example, it is traditional for all officers in some units to participate in PT quite early in the morning, yet often the child-care center does not open until a later time. One woman officer said:

> The child-care center opens at 6:30, but that's when PT starts. Dual [military] spouses or single parents find it is too difficult, because they are working on base. They have commitments, like they have to be at the rifle range at 4:30 a.m., and if your husband is gone TDY[18] or deployed, what can you do? There should be the availability to child care and flexibility. They need to allow officers to do what they are required to do. Getting a spot in day care on the base is hard; finding outside day care that meets those hours is very difficult.

---

[18]Temporary duty.

Typical of our dialogues, this woman did not expect to be released from her duties. Instead, she was looking for the day care that would allow her to fulfill her duty requirements.

Military Spouse Considerations

Frequent reassignments are typical and, by and large, expected for an officer. Officers demonstrate breadth in their careers by accepting assignments that vary both substantively and geographically. The best career moves can require an officer to move across the country or world. As a result, officers or their spouses must either suffer interruptions in their career development or couples must put up with lengthy separations. This burden seems to fall disproportionately on women. One-quarter of all women officers have reported that their spouse's job interferes with their military job, while only 15 percent of male officers with employed spouses have found their spouse's job interferes with their military job.[19] This problem is magnified by the fact that women officers are considerably more likely than their male peers to have an employed spouse. Only a small number of married men or women officers are geographically separated from their spouse at a particular point in time,[20] yet married women officers are more than four times as likely as their male peers to be "geographic bachelors" (5.8 percent as opposed to 1.3 percent).[21]

Some women in our study felt that partners who are on active duty are more familiar with and understanding of the demands of military life than are civilian partners. This may be one reason why women officers are more likely to marry other active-duty personnel. Yet

---

[19] 1992 Surveys of Officer and Enlisted Personnel (DMDC, 1993). This is the proportion that report that their spouse's job interferes "somewhat," "a great deal," or "completely" with their military career. Bielby and Bielby (1992) have found that civilian couples are less likely to make geographic moves for a woman's career opportunities than for a man's career opportunities even when the relative costs to the spouse's situation are equivalent. Nevertheless, Marsden et al. (1993) find that there is little difference in organizational commitment between men and women.

[20] While the number of officers who are separated from their spouse at any point in time is quite low, it is likely that the number who have had to be separated at some time is much higher. Unfortunately, the available data do not allow us to measure the incidence of separation from one's spouse over a longer period.

[21] 1992 Survey of Officer and Enlisted Personnel (DMDC, 1993).

dual military career marriages can also be particularly stressful as they can also increase the likelihood of facing separations from one's spouse. The services have instituted policies designed to minimize this difficulty, yet both women and men in dual military couples report that it can be difficult to arrange two career-enhancing positions at the same location. Usually, one partner must accept a less than ideal assignment. Given the up-or-out competitive nature of the officer career-management system, accepting a lesser assignment, especially more than once, may substantially limit an officer's promotion competitiveness and, ultimately, time in the service. Even when a dual military couple has accepted one partner's career as dominant, finding co-located opportunities can be difficult.

In a recent survey officers in dual military marriages were asked what they would do if a future assignment required a long separation from their spouse. They were asked to indicate whether they would simply accept the assignment, leave the service, or have their spouse leave the service. Only slightly more men than women said they would accept separate assignments. Among the others, men and women differed in who they said would separate from the service to avoid the assignment. Women officers stated that they were much more likely to separate than have their spouse separate or simply accept the assignment. Male officers were also more likely to state that they would leave rather than cause their spouse to separate, although not by nearly as wide a margin as women did (see Figure 14).

More women than men whom we interviewed had spouses on active duty. Further, more married women than married men in our interviews placed their careers as subordinate to their partners' careers.[22] It is not surprising, then, that the difficulties driven by dual military career marriages were a more common topic of discussion in our focus groups with women than with men. Similar to other conflicts between career and family responsibilities, many women in dual military marriages felt they were being forced to choose between family and career. "I love the [service] like family, but my decision to stay is now on a day-to-day basis . . . I've already spent two and one-

---

[22]This was not universally true, however. Some of the women we interviewed saw their career as dominant, and some of the men saw their career as subordinate.

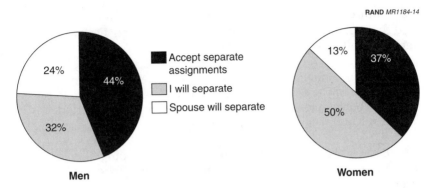

SOURCE: 1992 *Survey of Officer and Enlisted Personnel.*

Figure 14—"If Future Assignments Require Long Separations from Your Spouse, What Will You Do?"

half years separated from my husband and I'm facing the possibility of another separation."

ADVANTAGE IN THE SYSTEM

Some white men perceived that women carry an advantage in the career-management system. No black male officers who participated in our discussions agreed with this perception. The advantage, as perceived by some white men, results from personnel policies that explicitly treat women differently, principally the promotion goals in the board precepts. One white male officer stated, "If it's the male that can't keep up, he's gone. If it's the female, she won't necessarily be gone." Another commented, "The boards review the results, and if insufficient women and minorities are promoted, then white males get depromoted. I have noticed that on promotion boards, more incompetent women got promoted."

Many women recognized that some men believe women to be advantaged in the career-management system. A few women reported incidences where they believed this perception was used to justify not fully recognizing their performance. These women believed that their ranking officer awarded prized rating statuses to white male officers out of the belief that women would be promoted regardless and that white men needed the competitive boost. One woman offered the following experience:

> I got pulled into the office by my CO, who said, "You are augmented and you will be selected for Major, no problem; but we need to get these bubbas promoted. So even though you are the top performer, we will rank them up higher on the scale.

Another woman's superior told her that "he was going to take a lot of heat for giving both of the top ratings to the only two women in the group."

A small number of the women whom we interviewed believed that they had at times received an advantage in promotion consideration or in assignment consideration because of their gender. One woman commented:

> I have had to work harder to prove myself, but have been given the opportunity to do so perhaps more readily. For example, I think my recent promotion to O-5 has as much to do with being a woman as my performance.

While recognizing that being female may at times offer some advantage, nearly all women rejected outright the premise that *overall* they are advantaged in the career-management system. After considering all the factors discussed in this chapter, most women concluded that they must work harder than their male peers to receive similar recognition and reward. One female officer succinctly stated: "Women officers must be better than male counterparts to advance."

THE DOUBLE JEOPARDY OF BEING A BLACK WOMAN

It is apparent from the analysis in Chapter Three that the career progression of black women is the most divergent of the racial/gender groups studied. For the most part, black women did not express any unique issues during our discussions that were not also raised by either other women or other blacks. Further, there were no issues raised by white women or by black men that were not also raised by black women. Yet their experience and difficulties in career development *are* unique because both their race and gender simultaneously affect them. As a result many black women felt that they face a double disadvantage in their career development.

As our discussions with black women came to a close, we generally asked whether they felt their race or their gender had caused greater difficulties in their career. More black women in our discussions answered that being black had caused greater disadvantage than being female. In particular, black women focused on concerns related to social background and mentoring. The dialog in one group discussion reveals this concern:

> RAND Discussion Leader: To what extent are the difficulties you are reporting due to being female versus being black?

> Respondent 1: I think because of being a minority. My grandparents did not even finish high school. . . . No one told me 15 years ago you need to read certain things, read books, read the paper.

> Respondent 2: Or no one tells you how to establish a vision for your job, or about strategic thinking, etc.

> Respondent 3: [The majority] are taught that you need a vision. It's that mentoring. They are told, "You need to study Clausewitz."

However, the perspective that being a minority caused greater disadvantage than being a woman was not universally shared. One black officer commented: "Gender, to be female, causes more discrimination. Color causes people to prejudge, but not hate."

One final note on the "double jeopardy" of black women officers: Those white male officers who believed that the career-management system has instituted quotas for awarding promotions and other career advancements see black women as having two extra cards to lay on the table. One white male officer stated, "We're big boys, call the quota what it is, don't call it a goal. A black female is worth 50 white guys."

SUMMARY

As pointed out in Chapter Three, the key issue for understanding gender differences in career development and success is to understand why women officers choose to separate from the military at

substantially greater rates than do men. On the basis of both our research and the research of others, we conclude that this difference
derives from three broad issues: concentration in certain occupational specialties, lack of consensus among service members on the
role for women in the military, and competing family obligations.

Women officers continue to be concentrated in occupations with
more limited long-term career opportunities. While the concentration of women in support occupations appears to have little effect on
career opportunities through the O-4 level, noncombat occupational
specialties were clearly perceived by most officers participating in
this study to have limited opportunities to advance to the senior
ranks, O-6 and above. As a result many of the women saw their long-
term career opportunities as limited. It is too early to tell how these
perceptions will be changed by the 1993–94 policy change that
opened many occupations and assignments to women, especially in
the Navy and Air Force.

Several factors contributed to the belief expressed by many women
that their role in the military is not fully accepted. Substantial differences of opinion existed both between and among men and women
on whether it is appropriate for women to serve in any combat role,
including those currently open to women. Some women perceived
that the significant changes over the last decade in the occupational
and assignment restrictions for women have made it a particular
challenge to shape consistent and competitive career profiles. Some
women also saw the continued restrictions of women from certain
occupations as an institutional message reinforcing a view that
women are inherently less capable officers. Further, the sexual and
nonsexual harassment that many women reported adds to a sense
that some military personnel would prefer that women had no role in
the institution. Many women expressed weariness over their feeling
that they had to continually fight to be recognized, rewarded, and re-
spected for their role and accomplishments.

Finally, women officers face considerably different competing obligations from family responsibilities than do men. Married women
officers are more likely to have an employed spouse. While this alone
makes aggressive pursuit of a military career more difficult, adding
children to the equation makes the challenge even greater.

After weighing the questions of long-term career opportunities, the lack of full acceptance of their role by others and the institution, and conflicts with family responsibilities, many women concluded that the rewards of continued military service are less than the costs. That said, most women we interviewed expressed considerable pride in their military service and in the institutions. Most saw their military service as a positive experience, and many who intended to separate expressed regret that they found it necessary to end their military career.

Chapter Six

CONCLUSION

This study carried out two complementary research efforts to investigate the career progression of minority and women officers. First, we analyzed personnel data to measure retention and promotion by race/ethnicity and gender at each career stage, denoted by rank. By separating the years of service when retention decisions dominate from years when promotion selections are made, we uncovered differences that are hidden when the data are not structured in this way. Second, we sought out explanations for our quantitative findings and other information about career experiences by talking to officers in interviews and focus groups organized by minority and gender status.

The data analysis was carried out on seven cohorts between 1967 and 1991 and measured outcomes through promotion to O-6 (Colonel or Captain in the Navy). The analysis was structured to estimate differences between each minority/gender group and white males. There were no systematic differences in the patterns of minority and gender differences across services or cohorts. The interviews and focus groups involved midlevel officers chosen to represent all accession sources and occupations at one installation per service. We also interviewed officers who act as career managers to understand the policies and procedures by which assignments, command selections, and promotion boards are handled. Finally, we interviewed groups of senior officers who had recently served on O-5 and O-6 promotion boards to get insights on how the boards operate and what qualifications are considered to be most important.

SUMMARY OF FINDINGS

Our early data explorations showed career-progression patterns that differed by race/ethnicity *and* gender. Therefore, unlike other studies, we compared outcomes across four groups—white men, minority men, white women, and minority women—instead of two groups at a time—whites versus minorities or men versus women. For the most part, within the minority groups we focused on blacks; the populations of other minorities proved too small and too diverse to study in the same way. Where we could measure career outcomes for this group, they tended to fall between the career outcomes we measured for whites and blacks.

Overall, black male officers in the cohorts we studied were less likely than white males to be promoted and more likely to remain in service between promotions. There were few exceptions to this pattern in the nine career stages we evaluated. These differences offset one another, so overall about the same fraction of black and white male officers survived to career status at O-4. If, as suggested by most of the white officers we interviewed, blacks leave voluntarily for lucrative civilian jobs, we would have expected to see fewer blacks staying through retention periods. We did not see such a pattern of differences. Further, survey data indicate that similar fractions of black and white men expect to leave service to pursue civilian opportunities. Our data did not allow us to evaluate another explanation advanced by whites in our interviews and focus groups—that blacks enter service less well prepared. Other research suggests that blacks may be less well prepared, but this does not completely explain the gap between white and black promotion rates. However, in our interviews and focus groups, many white men did question the preparation of black officers, who in turn reported feeling a disproportionate need to prove themselves.

Our discussions with officers of both races point to the importance of social factors. Black men often reported that they did not have the peer and mentoring relationships that are important to success and in integrating socially. They also felt they were less likely to get plum assignments. The net result appears to be that black men felt that they have a harder time building competitive performance records to be considered by promotion boards. However, nearly all black male and black and white female officers believed that, given the materials available for their consideration, the promotion boards are fair.

White female officers were promoted at almost the same rate as their white male peers, but they were more likely to leave voluntarily between promotion periods. Our discussions with officers suggested that there are several reasons why women have left. First, past policies have kept women out of those combat-related occupations and assignments that are thought to lead to high rank. These policies were significantly changed while our research was under way, but the changes had yet to be widely felt. In addition, both men and women disagreed about the ultimate role for women, in particular whether they should serve in ground-combat units. Many women also reported they had experienced some level of sexual or nonsexual harassment and had been tested in ways that men weren't. In sum, many of the midcareer women with whom we talked were frustrated by the lack of clear roles and career paths, the differential treatment they received, and the difficulty in combining career and family. Like women in other demanding careers, some were opting out.

Black female officers were the least likely to be promoted at all stages. They were more likely than black men, but less likely than white women, to leave voluntarily in the years before they are considered for promotion to O-4. Almost the same fraction of black women and white women in a cohort attained the rank of O-4. However, like black men, black women were far more likely to leave at promotion stages than at retention stages. In our discussions with black women, they described themselves as doubly disadvantaged in the same ways as black men *and* white women.

Both white and black women with families found it hard to arrange day care and felt that their jobs interfered unnecessarily with family at times. Similarly, men also reported conflicts between career and family, but our discussions and DoD survey data indicate that these conflicts are more severe for women.

Other minority officers could be assessed only in the earlier career stages and through analysis of their promotion records but not through discussions in focus groups and interviews. Overall, their retention and promotion patterns resembled those of their African American counterparts.

What do these results indicate about the reasons for the "racial gap" and "gender gap" between junior and senior officers shown in the introduction to this report? The finding that about the same number of black and white men reached O-4 implies that racial diversity in the career years has been determined by the racial diversity in the entering cohort and that the current "racial gap" between junior and senior officers largely reflects the increase in black accessions over time. A closer look reveals persistent racial differences (for women as well as men) in promotion. These differences, which are offset by higher voluntary retention between promotions, need to be better understood. In contrast, some of the "gender gap" between junior and senior ranks is a result of retention differences between women and men, not just changes in the gender mix at accession.

In general, minority and female officers described themselves as facing some unique difficulties in building the competitive records of performance needed for promotion, especially to higher ranks. These difficulties result from differences in individual characteristics, social integration, and career-management policies. However, the specific problems minorities and women described to us differed in some respects. Academic preparation, social integration, mentoring, and assignments were seen as problematic for blacks. Family issues, changing roles, social integration, mentoring, harassment, and assignments were mentioned for women. All of these were mentioned for black women.

OFFICERS' SUGGESTIONS FOR CHANGE

Few of the problems officers described can be easily remedied, and many of them are echoed in the literature on minorities and women in the civilian workplace. Understanding this, the minority and female officers we talked to believed that they would fare no better, and might well be worse off, in a civilian job. Nevertheless, when asked, they did suggest some broad changes that they thought might improve opportunities for minority and female officers in the future. The most common suggestions were:

- Recruit more women and minorities into the officer corps and into underrepresented occupations. The minority and female officers we talked to typically mentioned this first when asked for suggestions. These officers believed that many of the obstacles they have faced resulted from their standing out in units predominantly staffed with white males. Making the officer corps more diverse is an obvious fix. However, the officers had few suggestions for how to attract more minorities and women. Black officers thought that it would be necessary to reach back into high schools and neighborhood groups to increase the number of black officers.

- Better inform all officers about career-management policies, especially those dealing with race and gender. Very few of the officers in our discussions said that they knew what the policies regarding minorities and women actually were, or how promotion boards work. We found these accurately described in the materials about careers that are now provided to officers, but active outreach may be needed to dispel the myths we encountered about affirmative action policies.[1]

- Avoid atypical assignment policies wherever possible. Fitting in all the assignments and education necessary for advancement is difficult, and other assignments make this even more difficult. Disproportionately assigning minorities and women to jobs, such as recruiting or equal opportunity, where diversity is highly valued also removes them from operational units where they can mentor younger officers. To conserve active-duty manpower, the Army is evaluating the use of reserve and retired personnel as ROTC instructors; this would eliminate at least one of the non-occupational demands for minority and female officers.

- Ensure that the criteria for assigning individuals to occupations and assignments are appropriate and applied equally to all officers.

Some of the suggestions focused on women's issues:

- Reevaluate the content and frequency of harassment training. The women we interviewed felt that current training programs were counterproductive because they led their male coworkers

---

[1]A recent article in *Army Times* (Tice, 1997) provides the kind of information needed.

to distance themselves and generally created an uncomfortable working environment for women.

- Develop more effective mechanisms for handling harassment complaints within the chain of command. Very few women are prepared to file formal complaints, for fear of damaging their own or the offender's career. There is a strong preference for working within the chain of command. Suggestions included assigning responsibility for harassment and other complaints within the command and holding commanders responsible for the working environment for minorities and women.

- Encourage practices that better accommodate families. Suggestions included expanding day care hours (as some commercial firms do) and avoiding clearly unnecessary off-hours duties. Although women most often focused on this issue, men also would welcome these changes. Those who suggested changes in time demands were emphatic that they didn't expect or want changes that would interfere with their unit's performance and readiness.

- Settle the role for women in the military. The women we interviewed expressed different views about what the role should be, but they all wanted their role to be settled and accepted.

An evaluation of these suggestions was beyond the scope of this study. We note that, with regard to increasing the numbers of minorities and women, it may also be possible to expand the enlisted commissioning programs in the future. The services are looking for ways to recruit an increasing number of young people with some college education and to provide enlisted personnel with the opportunity to pursue their education in service (Asch and Kilburn, 1999). If successful, these programs would increase the pool of individuals eligible for the commissioning programs.

All of the services have put considerable information about officer career-management policies and practices on the Internet, which most officers have ready access to even if deployed. However, this information still needs to be brought to young officers' attention. One method that appears to have been successful has senior officers who have served on promotion boards brief their commands on the process.

Many of the other suggestions relate to actions taken at the local level or to circumstances that vary across units. For example, with the pace of activity increasing in recent years (Hosek and Totten, 1998), family issues are of increasing concern. However, the impact on families of personnel working long hours at home is different from the impact on families of personnel who face a long deployment. There are programs to lessen these impacts, but to be effective they must be tailored to the needs of the personnel at each location. Similarly, policies for dealing with harassment are only as good as their implementation within the chain of command, where officers thought these problems should be dealt with. The Office of the Secretary of Defense (OSD) and the services can play a valuable role by setting clear objectives for local commanders and periodically monitoring the extent to which these objectives are being met.

PERFORMANCE EVALUATION PROCEDURES BY SERVICE

ARMY

At the time of this study, the Army evaluation system had been in use since 1979, more than twice as long as any previous system. There is general agreement that the then-current system was inflated to the point that its use in the promotion process was in question. As a result, revisions to the current evaluation form were under way.[1]

Performance evaluations are recorded on the Officer Evaluation Report (OER). The OER requires raters to evaluate an officer using a one to five scale on a number of performance factors: professionalism, job knowledge, physical fitness, communication skills, military bearing and appearance, ability to motivate subordinates, judgment, candor and frankness, responsiveness in stress situations, professional ethics (dedication, responsibility, loyalty, discipline, integrity, moral courage, selflessness, and moral standards), and support for equal opportunity. The rater must then indicate an overall assessment of performance and potential on a four-point scale.

An intermediate rater, when used, reinforces or amplifies areas of performance that he or she has personally observed. The senior rater provides both written comments and an overall rating of the officer. The written comments assess potential, performance at higher levels of responsibility, and promotion/education recommendations. The

---

[1]After this study was completed, a new evaluation form was adopted.

overall rating ranks the officer on a scale of one to nine. Promotion boards are provided with a senior rater's "profile" of overall rankings to put a rating in appropriate context. The profile presents the distribution of past rating scores that the rater has given. Officers may request a senior rater's profile, but the profile is not automatically appended to an officer's OER.

Many believe that the system does a poor job of differentiating between performance across officers. Ratings have inflated over time, with most officers now being rated in the top blocks. Further, the written comments also tend to be inflated. Army promotion board members indicated that they find signals for exceptional performance by searching for certain key phrases or words.

NAVY

Officers receive regular performance evaluations in the form of fitness reports—called FITREPs. There are three types of reports: regular, concurrent, and special. Regular FITREPs are submitted annually or upon the detachment of the officer or his/her reporting senior from an assignment. Concurrent reports are made by a second reporting senior on an officer away at school or on temporary additional duty, for instance. Special reports are made for a specific event or period of time, when the officer's performance warrants mention, whether positive or negative.

The FITREP includes a description of the current duties and responsibilities of the officer, a physical readiness rating, a performance rating, comments describing the officer's performance, a competitive ranking that measures the officer's performance in comparison to other officers being evaluated by the reporting senior, and a promotion recommendation.

Like all the services, the Navy has periodically revised its performance evaluation system in an attempt to reduce rating inflation as well as to achieve greater objectivity or otherwise enhance the evaluation process. The current FITREP came into use in 1995.

The Navy's new FITREP requires the rater to evaluate an officer on seven performance traits (but no personal traits). Evaluations are made on a five-point scale, ranging from "below standards" to "greatly exceeds standards." The seven trait grades are arithmetically averaged to provide a single overall score. The old form required the senior rater to provide a ranking of each officer relative to the other officers reviewed by the senior rater (e.g., second of five). In contrast, there is no relative ranking on the new FITREP.

Several guidelines have been adopted to direct the written general comments. First, all 5.0 and 1.0 scores must be substantiated with written comments. No relative numerical rankings are permitted, and all comments "must be verifiable." The form must be typed in a standard format and both highlighted type and handwritten comments are prohibited. As the grades in the old FITREPs became inflated, Navy FITREP writers began to use these methods to emphasize certain written remarks, as a way to indicate exceptional performance.

Finally, the form includes a promotion recommendation, which can be marked "not observed," "significant problems," "progressing," "promotable," "must promote," and "early promote." Early promote recommendations are limited to 20 percent of each summary group, and the combined total of early and must promote recommendations is limited to 50 percent of each summary group at the O-3 and O-4 levels and 40 percent at the O-5 and O-6 levels. Promotion recommendations (including early promotion) can be made even for officers not yet eligible for promotion; in other words, an officer not yet eligible for an early, or below-the-zone, promotion may still be rated promote early simply to indicate the reporting senior's high opinion of the officer. These changes in FITREPs are expected to reduce inflation and lead to greater fairness and ease of interpretation, at least for a while.

AIR FORCE

Performance is evaluated on the Officer Performance Report (OPR) first by the officer's immediate supervisor (the *rater*) and then by the supervisor's superior (the *additional rater*), who usually must be at least one grade senior to the officer being rated. The OPR undergoes a quality-control review by a senior officer (the *reviewer*), who adds comments only if he/she disagrees with the rating. The reviewer is the wing commander or equivalent for lieutenants through majors and the first general officer in the chain of command for lieutenant colonels and colonels.

The OPR includes a description of the unit mission, the job, and the officer's significant achievements in the job. Six performance factors are evaluated as either "meets standards" or "does not meet standards." The factors are job knowledge, leadership skills, professional qualities, organizational skills, judgment and decisions, and communication skills. Finally, the rater and the additional rater each provide their assessment of the officer's performance, and the reviewer indicates whether he or she concurs.

Between OPRs, supervisors are required to provide interim feedback to their officers through a handwritten Performance Feedback Worksheet and a face-to-face meeting. Recently, the Air Force required that the supervisors sign the form to indicate that this session occurred. The worksheet includes a rating for each component of the six factors rated in the OPR, using a continuous scale labeled "needs little improvement" at one end and "needs significant improvement" at the other end. There is also space for comments on the ratings. The comments are intended to clarify problems, give specific examples, and provide any other suggestions or assessments. These feedback sessions are intended to be an important component of the evaluation system.

The OPR is augmented by the Promotion Recommendation Form (PRF), which is completed 60 days before the officer is considered for promotion in or above the zone; a fraction of those who are below the zone also receive a PRF. The senior rater at the time—the same individual as the reviewer on the OPR—completes this form, which includes the same descriptions and narratives as the OPR and a recommendation to definitely promote, promote, or not promote based on the officer's cumulative record.[2] The number of officers who can be given a definitely promote recommendation is limited to a fraction less than the fraction who will be promoted. In addition, 10–15 percent of the below-the-zone candidates can be given a definitely promote recommendation. Senior raters forward their PRFs to an evaluation board consisting of senior raters from the numbered Air

---

[2]If the officer has recently been reassigned, the senior rater for the previous assignment completes the PRF.

Force, major commands, or headquarters organization level. This evaluation board is responsible for allocating all definitely promote recommendations for small units and the remaining definitely promote recommendations from rounding down the allocations to larger units. The PRF is destroyed after the promotion board for which it is prepared.

MARINE CORPS

Like the Navy, Marine Corps performance evaluations are also referred to as FITREPs. There are four types of Marine Corps FITREPs: regular, concurrent, academic, and special. Regular reports are given semiannually and also whenever the officer is detached, changes duty, or is promoted, and whenever the officer's reporting senior changes. Concurrent and special reports serve the same purposes as they do in the Navy.

The immediate commanding officer or head of the staff section generally serves as the officer's evaluator, or reporting senior. The reporting senior grades the officer on performance (regular and additional duties, handling of officers, handling of enlisted personnel, training personnel, tactical handling of troops) and qualities (endurance, personal appearance, military presence, attention to duty, cooperation, initiative, judgment, presence of mind, force, leadership, loyalty, personal relations, economy of management, and growth potential). Grades range from below average to outstanding; reporting seniors may assign a "not observed" score for any category in which the reporting senior feels his or her observation has been limited.[3]

The FITREP also asks the reporting senior to express his or her willingness "to have this Marine under your command . . . considering the requirements of *service in war*" (emphasis added) and asks for an indication of commendatory, adverse, or disciplinary action to which the officer was subject. A narrative section instructs the reporting senior to appraise the officer's professionalism.

---

[3]After this study was completed, the Marine Corps changed its evaluation report. The format, including the categories of performance graded, are now different.

Finally, a reviewing officer, typically the reporting senior's commanding officer, reviews the FITREP; he or she certifies that he or she
either has had no opportunity to observe the officer or concurs/does
not concur with the reporting senior's ranking and evaluation of the
officer. A new ranking is given if there is nonconcurrence with the
ranking given by the reporting senior. The reviewing officer is asked
to state the ranking of the officer relative to all officers of similar rank
whom he or she reviews. The reviewing officer may add narrative
remarks; such remarks are required if a *do not concur* is given.

INSTRUCTIONS TO PROMOTION AND OTHER SELECTION BOARDS REGARDING MINORITIES AND WOMEN

DoD Directive 1320.12 requires that the instructions to promotion boards include "guidelines to ensure the board considers all eligible officers without prejudice or partiality." The instructions are prepared by the service secretaries and included the following language at the time of this study.

ARMY[1]

"a.   The Army is firmly committed to providing equal opportunity for minority and female officers in all facets of their career development, utilization, and progression. In evaluating the records of minority and female officers, the board should consider that past personal and institutional discrimination might have disadvantaged minority and female officers. Such discrimination may manifest itself in disproportionately lower evaluation reports, assignments of lesser importance or responsibility, etc. Take these factors into consideration in evaluating these officers' potential to make continued significant contributions to the Army.

b.   The goal for this board is to achieve a percentage of minority and female selections not less than the selection rate for all officers in the promotion zone (first-time considered category). This goal is important because, to the extent that each board achieves it, the

---

[1] This guidance was replaced effective 28 September 1999.

Army at large will have a clear perception of equal opportunity and the selectees will enjoy continued career progression to the benefit of the Army.

c.   Prior to adjournment, the board must review the extent to which it met this goal and explain the reasons for any failure to meet this goal in the report of officers recommended for promotion. Although the board may have met the overall selection goals for minorities and women, it will identify any situation in which minority or female selections were not comparable to the overall population in specific branches or where a particular minority-gender grouping did not fare well in comparison to the overall population. Explain such situations fully in the after-action report."

NAVY AND MARINE CORPS[2]

Since they share a Secretariat, board instructions are the same. The Precept says:

"The board's evaluation of women and minority officers must afford them fair and equitable consideration."

This statement is backed up with a much longer section in the supplemental guidance to the board members:

"The Department of the Navy is dedicated to equality of treatment and opportunity for all personnel without regard to race, creed, color, gender, or national origin. Aggressive commitment to equal opportunity is critical. Invidious discrimination is not only morally wrong but it is illegal. You must not let it play a role in your deliberations or affect your consideration of individual officers.

a.   As stated previously, the board's evaluation of women and minority officers must afford them fair and equitable consideration. In evaluating the records of women and minority officers, you should be alert to the possibility that past discrimination may have placed these officers at a disadvantage in the Performance Evaluation System. In some instances, utilization policies, such as

---

[2]This language was subsequently modified.

the statutory and regulatory restrictions on the assignment of women, and assignment practice may have resulted in the involuntary assignment of women and minority officers outside traditional career development patterns, i.e., to equal opportunity, human resource, family service, and similar billets. These assignments, though beneficial to the interests of the Navy [Marine Corps], have produced some women and minority officers with career patterns different from officers who have been able to serve in their primary specialties. These assignments must be viewed as equally beneficial to the Navy and performance in such assignments should be given the same weight as that given to duty equally well performed by officers serving in their primary specialties.

b.   Despite considerable progress in ensuring fair treatment of minority officers, these officers historically have not been promoted at rates equivalent to those of other officers. This has been more evident in the case of African Americans than other minority groups. Previous studies on equal opportunity in the military have noted that, prior to entering the Service, some minority officers have had limited interaction with a predominantly majority environment. Consequently, minority officers may take a longer time to adjust and perform to the level of their contemporaries. This may result in initially lower fitness reports at the junior officer level (through O-3) and a higher percentage of "late bloomers" when evaluating potential and in determining which eligible officers are best and fully qualified for promotion.

c.   Within the charter of "best and fully qualified," the Navy goal is to attain a minority selection rate at a minimum equal to the overall selection rate. This goal is important because the Navy benefits by ensuring the talents of minority officers are not overlooked because of the officers' past assignments, precommissioning social background, or possibly biased fitness reports. Prior to adjournment, the board must review the extent to which the goal of equivalent selection rates has been met."

AIR FORCE

"Your evaluation of minority and some officers must clearly afford them fair and equitable consideration. Equal opportunity for all officers is an essential element of our selection system. In your evaluation of the records of minority and women officers, you should be

particularly sensitive to the possibility that past individuals and societal attitudes, and in some instances utilization policies or practices, may have placed these officers at a disadvantage from a total
career perspective. The board shall prepare for review by the
Secretary and Chief of Staff, a report of minority and women officer
selections as compared to the selection rates for all officers considered by the board."

DETAILED DESCRIPTION OF PROMOTION AND RETENTION DATA ANALYSIS

OFFICER COHORT FILES AND VARIABLE DEFINITIONS

As discussed briefly in Chapter Three, the longitudinal data set used in the statistical analysis in this report was created specifically for this study by DMDC. In this appendix, we provide more details about these data and about how we created some of the variables used in the analysis.

The data DMDC created included officers who assessed in 1967, 1970, 1977, 1980, 1983, 1987, 1991, and 1994. DMDC also provided data for 1973, but we did not use these data due to clear errors in many of the important fields. A record for each officer included the first 95 bytes of the officer's Master File record[1] for each year the officer was in the service. Master File records are available beginning in 1977. Hence, we observed all years of service for individuals who entered in 1977 or later, but for individuals who entered before 1977, we only observed records for 1977 or later. The first 95 bytes of the Master File contain the following variables: total active federal military service, DoD primary occupation group, DoD duty occupation group, education, pay grade, home of record, date of birth, service, race, source of commission, marital status, number of dependents, ethnic group, race/ethnicity, sex, enlisted years of service, DoD secondary occupation code, age at entry, current age, primary military

---

[1]See DMDC (2000) for more information regarding the Master File.

occupational specialty (MOS), basic active service date, expected term of service date, date of current rank, date of entry to current rank, component, year of active duty service, months in grade, pay entry base date, location, unit identification code, Spanish surname flag, duty MOS, and unit Zip code.

In our analysis we included a variable that indicates the officer's occupation. This variable is the officer's 1-digit DoD occupational code[2] for the primary military occupational specialty to which he or she was assigned in his or her fourth year. If an officer did not survive to the fourth year, we used the last observation of occupation. For officers in the 1967 and 1977 cohorts, we used the first observed occupation. We obtained the occupation from the fourth year because we found that many officers were in student, training, or unassigned occupation categories in earlier years during periods when they might still be training for their occupational specialty. We found that while many officers changed assignments over time, almost all of them stayed in the same 1-digit DoD category. Hence, we did not create occupational categories that changed over time, but rather used the occupation in the fourth year of service.

We created a variable to indicate whether an officer had prior service experience, presumably as an enlisted person. To create this variable, we compared the total active military service to the current years of service variable. Total active military service (TAFMS) indicates the number of years of service a servicemember has accumulated toward retirement eligibility. The current years of service (CYOS) variable indicates the number of years a person has been an officer. If TAFMS is greater than CYOS, we assumed the officer had some prior service experience.

We created the promotion and retention variables according to schedules of promotion for each cohort and service that we identified in the data. Recall that we created a promotion variable for each promotion that takes a value of one if the person was in the military in the period when the person was eligible for promotion—presumably shortly after the promotion board met—and we observed his or her rank progressing one level. The retention variable equals one if

---

[2]Consult the Occupational conversion manual for a description of these codes.

the person was present in the promotion eligibility period and either a) we did not observe that person achieving a higher rank, or b) the person left the military during the period the board met.

The promotion schedules we identified from the data indicated the period when a cohort's promotions occurred. For each cohort and service, we created a promotion schedule by observing when individuals in that cohort and service got each promotion. Approximately 95 percent of promotions to a specific rank in our data took place within one year—the modal year—of all other promotions to that rank for a given cohort and service. We designated the period including the year before the modal year to the year after the modal year as being the period when the individual was eligible for promotion. For some of the earlier promotions, we observed nearly all of the promotions occurring within a two-year window rather than a three-year window, and so we only used two years as the period of eligibility rather than three years.

The promotion schedules were critical for creating the retention variables as well. Only individuals who were still in the service the year after the promotion eligibility window were given a retention value. Given that the person was promoted and present the year after the promotions took place, the person was given a value of one if he or she was still in the service the first year of the next promotion eligibility period. This value indicates that the person stayed in the service the entire period from being promoted to one rank to being at risk to receive the next promotion. The person received a value of zero if he or she was not in the service when the next promotion board met. That is, the person received the previous promotion, but did not stay in the service long enough to be at risk to get the next promotion.

CHANGES IN RACE AND ETHNICITY IDENTIFICATION OVER TIME

Reflecting trends in civilian data collection, collection of race and ethnicity information by the military has evolved over time. In both officer and enlisted files, the military now collects information on both race and ethnicity. Individuals, or sometimes recruiters or other administrators,[3] indicate whether the person is black, white, or belongs to another racial group, which is designated "other." In addition, individuals report whether they belong to one of 20 ethnic groups that include five Hispanic groups, three Native American or Eskimo groups, seven Asian groups, four Pacific Islander groups, and one other/none category. Using the answers to these questions, the military creates a race/ethnicity variable that classifies individuals as being non-Hispanic white, non-Hispanic black, Hispanic, American Indian, Asian/Pacific Islander, or other.[4]

Not only has the organization changed its collection of race and ethnicity information over time but also individuals in the military appear to have changed the way they self-report race and ethnicity. Again, this parallels trends in the civilian sector (see discussion in Appendix K of National Research Council, 1995). In 1980, we observe 73 percent of individuals who self-identify as being Hispanic reported that they are of white race and 25 percent reported they are other race when race choices are white, black, or other. In contrast, by 1991, 56 percent of officers who report being Hispanic indicated that their race is white while 41 percent reported that their race is other. Note that less than 3 percent of Hispanics in all years reported being black. Other ethnic groups—American Indian, Asian/Pacific Islander, and other—also exhibited the same decline in the fraction reporting white race and increase in the fraction reporting other race.

This change in the way Hispanics and other ethnic groups self-identify has implications for our analysis. Primarily, in the earlier years of the data, a larger fraction of individuals in the "white" group will be Hispanic or belong to other ethnic groups. Concomitantly, in later years, the "other" group will include more individuals who consider themselves to belong to one of the ethnic groups. In other words, the white comparison group is becoming less ethnically diverse over the period of our analysis. The "other" group is becoming larger over the period both because the numbers of minorities have increased and

---

[3]Personal communication with MSGT Ed Zapanta of DMDC.

[4]Before 1979 the ethnic group and race/ethnicity categories were slightly different. See Master File documentation for details. This change does not influence our analysis.

also because more individuals who previously would have self-identified as being white were in the "other" category.

While the ethnic composition of the white and other racial groups we analyze changed over the period of our analysis, we observe little change in the ethnicity of individuals who reported that their race is black. This implies that the ethnic composition of the black racial group is relatively stable over the period.

Given this information as background, we will now discuss why we limited our statistical analysis to the comparison of the three racial groups—black, white, and other—rather than also examining other minority groups such as Asians, Hispanics, or other groups. Recall that Hispanics can be of any race. In 1994, approximately 60 percent were classified as white and 37 percent were classified as other race. In models containing a Hispanic dummy variable, we rarely found significant differences from whites. This is probably explained by the fact that such large fractions of Hispanics are whites. We tested for differences in non-Hispanic whites and Hispanic whites and found no difference. Our sample sizes of non-Hispanic and Hispanic individuals of other race were too small to conduct meaningful comparisons of these groups to other groups. Due to these results, we decided not to include Hispanics as a comparison group in our analysis.

We also considered the possibility of examining outcomes for other racial minorities including Asians, etc. The sample sizes of these subgroups of the "other" racial group were too small to conduct statistical comparisons. As a result, we collapsed these categories into the race category "other."

DETAILED REGRESSION RESULTS

We report the complete set of regression results in Tables C.2–C.21 at the end of the appendix and discuss other details of the estimation in this appendix. In addition to the specifications reported here, we also estimated a number of other specifications. As reported in the discussion of race and ethnicity, we estimated models that included a Hispanic variable.

As reported in Chapter Three, we considered the possibility that minority or gender differences in career progression varied in systematic ways by service or cohort. We examined this possibility by estimating separate models for each service or cohort. While we sometimes found different estimates of the minority or gender effects in these various models, we did not observe any consistent patterns whereby minorities or women experienced consistently different career progression in a particular service or cohort (Table C.1).

Another specification we examined included marital status as one of the explanatory variables. While marital status is clearly an endogenous variable, we were simply interested in the question of whether there were any differences in career progression by marital status. We included variables that indicated whether an individual was married, single, or of unknown marital status at the time of a particular career transition. We also included interactions of these variables and being female to ascertain whether marital status had different implications for career progression for male and female officers. We were able to obtain results for these models only in the earliest stages of the career because of cell size limitations: So few male officers were single that it was not possible to differentiate between single officers and single female officers. For example, for the 1980 cohort, when they were at risk to be promoted to O-4, 26 percent of male officers were single while 40 percent of female officers were single.

In the models for which we did have sufficient numbers of officers in each cell, the coefficient on the married indicator is positive and significant for both retention and promotion models. For the married and female interaction, in promotion models (Prom12 and Prom23 only) the estimate is significant and negative, but not larger than the estimate of the married indicator. This implies that married male officers on net are more likely to be promoted than are single male officers and that married female officers are also more likely to be promoted than single female officers, but that the marriage premium is smaller for females than for males. In retention models (Stay 2 and Stay 3 only), the married indicator is also positive and significant and the married female interaction is also negative and significant. However, for the retention models, the negative married female interaction is larger than the married indicator estimate. This

Table C.1

Minority/Gender Differences in Retention and Promotion
by Cohort and Service
(Black Males/White Females)

Window	Cohort						
	1967	1970	1977	1980	1983	1987	1991
Retention							
O-2			ns/ns	ns/-	ns/-	ns/-	
O-3			+/-	+/-			
O-4	-/ns	ns/ns	ns/+				
O-5	+/ns	ns/ns					
Promotion							
O-1–O-2			-/ns	-/-	-/-	ns/-	-/-
O-2–O-3			ns/-	-/-	ns/-	ns/-	
O-3–O-4			-/+	ns/+			
O-4–O-5	-/ns	ns/ns					
O-5–O-6	ns/ns	ns/ns					

Window	Service			
	Army	Navy	Marines	Air Force
Retention				
O-2	+/-	-/+	-/ns	ns/-
O-3	+/-	ns/+	ns/ns	+/-
O-4	ns/ns	ns/ns	ns/ns	ns/ns
O-5	+/ns	ns/ns	ns/ns	ns/ns
Promotion				
O-1–O-2	-/-	ns/-	-/-	-/-
O-2–O-3	ns/-	-/ns	-/ns	ns/-
O-3–O-4	ns/ns	-/+	-/-	ns/+
O-4–O-5	-/ns	ns/-	ns/ns	ns/ns
O-5–O-6	ns/ns	ns/ns	ns/ns	ns/ns

NOTE: Cells that are blank denote regressions that could not be estimated due to small sample sizes.
+ =pos., stat signif.
- = neg., stat signif.
ns = not signif.

suggests that while married males are more likely than their single counterparts to stay in service between promotions, married females are less likely than their single counterparts to stay in between promotions.

The models we estimated are conditional on individuals in the analysis having achieved the previous grade. Hence, this implies that our results are representative of the likelihood that individuals will be promoted or retained given that they are at risk to make each particular transition. However, our results are not representative of the likelihood that all officers who access make these transitions.

We used two approaches to simulate the probability that individuals progress through a number of these transitions. First, for individuals we observed for a long enough period, we estimated the probability that entering officers attained grade O-4 (using 1977 and 1980 cohorts) and that officers who attained O-4 reached O-6 (using 1967 and 1970 cohorts). The results for these estimates summarize the differences in these two career segments for minority and gender groups in the included cohorts. Second, we simulated the cumulative differences in minority and gender group career progression by multiplying the differences in probabilities computed for each of the transitions required to achieve a particular grade. For example, to simulate the total difference between male and female probabilities in reaching O-4, we multiplied the difference in probability estimated for females in the promotion from O-1 to O-2, O-2 retention, the promotion from O-2 to O-3, O-3 retention, and the promotion from O-3 to O-4. While this exercise does not violate any of the rules of probability, it suffers from the flaw that the sequential transitions are not likely to be completely independent of each other. That is, the error terms of these probability models are likely to be correlated as in the seemingly unrelated regression (SUR) model (see Greene, 1993). However, given that we used the same set of regressors in each equation, our estimates will still be consistent. Unlike the typical SUR model, we did not have identical observations in each equation, so considering the correlation in the error terms might lead to more efficient estimates. Note that when we used the second method to calculate differences in reaching O-4 by race and gender, we obtained the same results we did when using the first method to estimate the rate of attaining O-4 (see Tables C.2–C.21).

Table C.2

Promotion O-1 to O-2
(Control for officer's entry path)

Variable	Parameter Estimate	Standard Error	Pr > Chi-Square
Intercept	3.6691	0.0831	0.0001
Prior Service	0.1087	0.0573	0.0576
Army			
Navy	2.9172	0.0890	0.0001
Marines	3.4379	0.1089	0.0001
Air Force	0.8216	0.0508	0.0001
Academy			
ROTC Scholarship	−0.6770	0.0853	0.0001
ROTC Regular	−1.6542	0.0772	0.0001
OCS/OTS	−1.3756	0.0849	0.0001
Direct Appointment	−1.7742	0.1073	0.0001
Unknown Accession	−1.0548	0.0991	0.0001
White Male			
Black Male	−0.4971	0.0635	0.0001
Other Male	−0.3777	0.1053	0.0003
White Female	−0.3651	0.0635	0.0001
Black Female	−0.7750	0.1083	0.0001
Other Female	−0.7495	0.2396	0.0018
Executive	−2.4124	1.0323	0.0195
Tactical Operations			
Intelligence	0.2439	0.0975	0.0124
Engineering/Maintenance	0.0487	0.0570	0.3928
Administration	−0.1386	0.0636	0.0293
Supply/Procurement	0.1922	0.0819	0.0189
Nonoccupational	−4.0817	0.0736	0.0001
Cohort 77			
Cohort 80	0.2246	0.0563	0.0001
Cohort 83	0.4404	0.0608	0.0001
Cohort 87	0.7182	0.0653	0.0001
Cohort 91	0.2908	0.0633	0.0001
	Promoted	Count	
	Yes	72733	
	No	3604	

Table C.3

Promotion O-2 to O-3
(Control for officer's entry path)

Variable	Parameter Estimate	Standard Error	Pr > Chi-Square
Intercept	3.0869	0.0600	0.0001
Prior Service	0.4732	0.0416	0.0001
Army			
Navy	0.4422	0.0382	0.0001
Marines	0.1842	0.0552	0.0008
Air Force	0.9736	0.0385	0.0001
Academy			
ROTC Scholarship	−1.4295	0.0550	0.0001
ROTC Regular	−0.9607	0.0577	0.0001
OCS/OTS	−1.4162	0.0568	0.0001
Direct Appointment	−0.6654	0.1097	0.0001
Unknown Accession	−0.7606	0.0628	0.0001
White Male			
Black Male	−0.2064	0.0550	0.0002
Other Male	−0.2745	0.0883	0.0019
White Female	−0.3234	0.0454	0.0001
Black Female	−0.3376	0.1022	0.0010
Other Female	−0.5291	0.2151	0.0139
Executive	0.8859	0.5165	0.0863
Tactical Operations			
Intelligence	−0.1239	0.0609	0.0420
Engineering/Maintenance	−0.6686	0.0345	0.0001
Administration	−0.4254	0.0437	0.0001
Supply/Procurement	−0.2030	0.0508	0.0001
Nonoccupational	−2.6472	0.0819	0.0001
Cohort 77			
Cohort 80	−0.2288	0.0393	0.0001
Cohort 83	−0.2932	0.0394	0.0001
Cohort 87	−0.1878	0.0435	0.0001

Promoted	Count
Yes	50020
No	6906

Table C.4

Promotion O-3 to O-4
(Control for officer's entry path)

Variable	Parameter Estimate	Standard Error	Pr > Chi-Square
Intercept	1.3217	0.0626	0.0001
Prior Service	−0.0555	0.0494	0.2616
Army			
Navy	0.3925	0.0563	0.0001
Marines	0.0847	0.0768	0.2698
Air Force	0.5394	0.0500	0.0001
Academy			
ROTC Scholarship	−0.1335	0.0699	0.0561
ROTC Regular	−0.4136	0.0663	0.0001
OCS/OTS	−0.4947	0.0689	0.0001
Direct Appointment	−0.4096	0.1145	0.0003
Unknown Accession	−0.3625	0.0801	0.0001
White Male			
Black Male	−0.2212	0.0725	0.0023
Other Male	−0.4210	0.1216	0.0005
White Female	0.2453	0.0749	0.0011
Black Female	−0.3377	0.1450	0.0199
Other Female	−0.1415	0.3886	0.7158
Executive	−0.0026	0.3441	0.9940
Tactical Operations			
Intelligence	0.0866	0.0823	0.2929
Engineering/Maintenance	−0.2457	0.0514	0.0001
Administration	−0.3750	0.0565	0.0001
Supply/Procurement	0.1475	0.0667	0.0269
Nonoccupational	−1.3378	0.3837	0.0005
Cohort 77			
Cohort 80	−0.1608	0.0384	0.0001
	Promoted	Count	
	Yes	12073	
	No	4103	

Table C.5

Promotion O-4 to O-5
(Control for officer's entry path)

Variable	Parameter Estimate	Standard Error	Pr > Chi-Square
Intercept	1.9334	0.0951	0.0001
Prior Service	−0.3741	0.0653	0.0001
Army			
Navy	−0.1208	0.0781	0.1219
Marines	−0.1396	0.0918	0.1285
Air Force	−0.2758	0.0572	0.0001
Academy			
ROTC Scholarship	−0.2253	0.1158	0.0517
ROTC Regular	−0.6252	0.0906	0.0001
OCS/OTS	−0.8081	0.0903	0.0001
Direct Appointment	−0.8267	0.1787	0.0001
Unknown Accession	−0.3705	0.1113	0.0009
White Male			
Black Male	−0.3014	0.1315	0.0219
White Female	−0.0234	0.1691	0.8899
Black Female	−0.8889	0.8261	0.2819
Executive	1.3276	0.5275	0.0119
Tactical Operations			
Intelligence	0.0694	0.1462	0.6351
Engineering/Maintenance	−0.2882	0.0807	0.0004
Administration	−0.0104	0.1046	0.9211
Supply/Procurement	0.0010	0.1178	0.9934
Cohort 67			
Cohort 70	−0.1564	0.0547	0.0042
Cohort 77			

	Promoted	Count	
	Yes	7811	
	No	2808	

Table C.6

Promotion O-5 to O-6
(Control for officer's entry path)

Variable	Parameter Estimate	Standard Error	Pr > Chi-Square
Intercept	0.6185	0.0928	0.0001
Prior Service	−0.2394	0.0876	0.0063
Army			
Navy	−0.0356	0.0809	0.6598
Marines	0.1479	0.1156	0.2009
Air Force	−0.2293	0.0712	0.0013
Academy			
ROTC Scholarship	−0.5295	0.1123	0.0001
ROTC Regular	−0.5886	0.0910	0.0001
OCS/OTS	−0.7650	0.0921	0.0001
Direct Appointment	−1.1281	0.2273	0.0001
Unknown Accession	−0.4920	0.1106	0.0001
White Male			
Black Male	0.2021	0.1712	0.2380
White Female	0.1337	0.2228	0.5483
Black Female	0.3033	1.4158	0.8304
Executive	0.9655	0.3083	0.0017
Tactical Operations			
Intelligence	−0.1920	0.1631	0.2392
Engineering/Maintenance	−0.2378	0.1099	0.0306
Administration	−0.1865	0.1197	0.1192
Supply/Procurement	0.7929	0.1145	0.0001
Cohort 67			
Cohort 70	0.0725	0.0643	0.2595
Cohort 77			

	Promoted	Count	
	Yes	2914	
	No	2886	

Table C.7

Promotion O-1 to O-2
(Do not control for officer's entry path)

Variable	Parameter Estimate	Standard Error	Pr > Chi-Square
Intercept	2.5882	0.0417	0.0001
Army			
Navy	1.0701	0.0556	0.0001
Marines	0.8965	0.0792	0.0001
Air Force	0.2208	0.0382	0.0001
Academy			
White Male			
Black Male	−0.4924	0.0596	0.0001
Other Male	−0.3476	0.0978	0.0004
White Female	−0.2697	0.0554	0.0001
Black Female	−0.7132	0.1018	0.0001
Other Female	−0.4618	0.2289	0.0436
Tactical Operations			
Cohort 77			
Cohort 80	0.3054	0.0523	0.0001
Cohort 83	0.3228	0.0522	0.0001
Cohort 87	0.3284	0.0566	0.0001
Cohort 91	−0.1465	0.0537	0.0063
	Promoted	Count	
	Yes	72733	
	No	3604	

Table C.8

Promotion O-2 to O-3
(Do not control for officer's entry path)

Variable	Parameter Estimate	Standard Error	Pr > Chi-Square
Intercept	1.9696	0.0341	0.0001
Army			
Navy	0.0847	0.0328	0.0097
Marines	0.0028	0.0496	0.9551
Air Force	0.7153	0.0332	0.0001
Academy			
White Male			
Black Male	−0.2279	0.0531	0.0001
Other Male	−0.1844	0.0850	0.0300
White Female	−0.4694	0.0422	0.0001
Black Female	−0.4632	0.0993	0.0001
Other Female	−0.5883	0.2102	0.0051
Tactical Operations			
Cohort 77			
Cohort 80	−0.1961	0.0380	0.0001
Cohort 83	−0.2228	0.0377	0.0001
Cohort 87	−0.2086	0.0402	0.0001
	Promoted	Count	
	Yes	50020	
	No	6906	

Table C.9

Promotion O-3 to O-4
(Do not control for officer's entry path)

Variable	Parameter Estimate	Standard Error	Pr > Chi-Square
Intercept	1.0017	0.0372	0.0001
Army			
Navy	0.3042	0.0500	0.0001
Marines	−0.0160	0.0732	0.8271
Air Force	0.4223	0.0432	0.0001
Academy			
White Male			
Black Male	−0.2976	0.0714	0.0001
Other Male	−0.4048	0.1206	0.0008
White Female	0.0767	0.0706	0.2773
Black Female	−0.5361	0.1418	0.0002
Other Female	−0.3978	0.3863	0.3031
Tactical Operations			
Cohort 77			
Cohort 80	−0.2005	0.0369	0.0001
	Promoted	Count	
	Yes	12073	
	No	4103	

Table C.10

Promotion O-4 to O-5
(Do not control for officer's entry path)

Variable	Parameter Estimate	Standard Error	Pr > Chi-Square
Intercept	1.2316	0.0461	0.0001
Army			
Navy	–0.0323	0.0741	0.6628
Marines	–0.2462	0.0878	0.0051
Air Force	–0.3233	0.0511	0.0001
Academy			
White Male			
Black Male	–0.3695	0.1298	0.0044
White Female	–0.1816	0.1635	0.2666
Black Female	–1.0919	0.8197	0.1828
Tactical Operations			
Cohort 67			
Cohort 70	–0.0386	0.0444	0.3853
Cohort 77			

	Promoted	Count	
	Yes	7812	
	No	2809	

Table C.11

Promotion O-5 to O-6
(Do not control for officer's entry path)

Variable	Parameter Estimate	Standard Error	Pr > Chi-Square
Intercept	0.0731	0.0537	0.1729
Army			
Navy	0.0742	0.0761	0.3295
Marines	0.0845	0.1100	0.4421
Air Force	−0.2367	0.0633	0.0002
Academy			
White Male			
Black Male	0.1037	0.1689	0.5393
White Female	−0.1030	0.2149	0.6318
Black Female	0.1286	1.4151	0.9276
Tactical Operations			
Cohort 67			
Cohort 70	0.0350	0.0531	0.5097
Cohort 77			

	Promoted	Count	
	Yes	2914	
	No	2886	

Table C.12

Entrants Who Attained O-4

Variable	Parameter Estimate	Standard Error	Pr > Chi-Square
Intercept	−0.3811	0.0384	0.0001
Prior Service	0.3733	0.0331	0.0001
Army			
Navy	0.1527	0.0359	0.0001
Marines	−0.1852	0.0503	0.0002
Air Force	0.5377	0.0317	0.0001
Academy			
ROTC Scholarship	−0.3018	0.0407	0.0001
ROTC Regular	−0.3369	0.0405	0.0001
OCS/OTS	−0.4689	0.0414	0.0001
Direct Appointment	−0.2769	0.0759	0.0003
Unknown Accession	−0.0907	0.0504	0.0720
White Male			
Black Male	−0.0942	0.0505	0.0619
Other Male	−0.2620	0.0863	0.0024
White Female	−0.3797	0.0442	0.0001
Black Female	−0.4048	0.1046	0.0001
Other Female	−0.6846	0.2552	0.0073
Executive	0.3826	0.2650	0.1488
Tactical Operations			
Intelligence	0.4519	0.0557	0.0001
Engineering/Maintenance	0.0471	0.0321	0.1421
Administration	0.2005	0.0363	0.0001
Supply/Procurement	0.2873	0.0486	0.0001
Nonoccupational	−0.1715	0.2090	0.4120
Cohort 77			
Cohort 80	−0.2488	0.0246	0.0001
	Attained O-4	Count	
	Yes	12073	
	No	19779	

Table C.13

O-4 Officers Who Attained O-6

Variable	Parameter Estimate	Standard Error	Pr > Chi-Square
Intercept	−0.8166	0.0673	0.0001
Prior Service	−0.8990	0.0685	0.0001
Army			
Navy	0.0952	0.0622	0.1260
Marines	0.0898	0.0865	0.2988
Air Force	−0.2128	0.0531	0.0001
Academy			
ROTC Scholarship	−0.2870	0.0826	0.0005
ROTC Regular	−0.4743	0.0663	0.0001
OCS/OTS	−0.7254	0.0679	0.0001
Direct Appointment	−0.9222	0.1870	0.0001
Unknown Accession	−0.3953	0.0813	0.0001
White Male			
Black Male	0.0947	0.1274	0.4571
White Female	0.0278	0.1764	0.8746
Black Female	−0.3978	1.0565	0.7065
Executive	−0.7232	0.4763	0.1289
Tactical Operations			
Intelligence	0.0631	0.0999	0.5274
Engineering/Maintenance	0.0327	0.0558	0.5582
Administration	−0.1079	0.0676	0.1106
Supply/Procurement	0.2890	0.0766	0.0002
Cohort 67			
Cohort 70	−0.4350	0.0425	0.0001
Cohort 77			

	Attained 0-6	Count
	Yes	2912
	No	15944

Table C.14

Retained During O-2
(Control for officer's entry path)

Variable	Parameter Estimate	Standard Error	Pr > Chi-Square
Intercept	2.8912	0.0683	0.0001
Prior Service	0.2352	0.0482	0.0001
Army			
Navy	1.8050	0.0584	0.0001
Marines	−0.4765	0.0472	0.0001
Air Force	2.7911	0.0707	0.0001
Academy			
ROTC Scholarship	0.3339	0.0876	0.0001
ROTC Regular	−1.1661	0.0633	0.0001
OCS/OTS	−1.5089	0.0680	0.0001
Direct Appointment	−0.6889	0.1110	0.0001
Unknown Accession	−1.1011	0.0688	0.0001
White Male			
Black Male	−0.0137	0.0620	0.8255
Other Male	0.0176	0.1122	0.8757
White Female	−0.3697	0.0556	0.0001
Black Female	−0.2435	0.1137	0.0322
Other Female	−0.4920	0.2617	0.0601
Executive	−0.4486	1.0332	0.6642
Tactical Operations			
Intelligence	0.1259	0.0812	0.1211
Engineering/Maintenance	−0.2653	0.0454	0.0001
Administration	−0.2220	0.0585	0.0001
Supply/Procurement	−0.3221	0.0539	0.0001
Nonoccupational	0.0601	0.0773	0.4364
Cohort 77			
Cohort 80	0.2397	0.0503	0.0001
Cohort 83	−0.0444	0.0489	0.3634
Cohort 87	−0.7073	0.0467	0.0001
	Retained	Count	
	Yes	56926	
	No	4911	

Table C.15

Retained During O-3
(Control for officer's entry path)

Variable	Parameter Estimate	Standard Error	Pr > Chi-Square
Intercept	0.5309	0.0417	0.0001
Prior Service	0.6274	0.0409	0.0001
Army			
Navy	−0.2180	0.0407	0.0001
Marines	−0.3668	0.0595	0.0001
Air Force	−0.0266	0.0364	0.4647
Academy			
ROTC Scholarship	0.1563	0.0432	0.0003
ROTC Regular	0.4957	0.0450	0.0001
OCS/OTS	0.3359	0.0453	0.0001
Direct Appointment	0.4227	0.0875	0.0001
Unknown Accession	0.5227	0.0566	0.0001
White Male			
Black Male	0.2921	0.0641	0.0001
Other Male	0.0155	0.0970	0.8729
White Female	−0.3104	0.0500	0.0001
Black Female	0.2184	0.1294	0.0916
Other Female	−0.0273	0.3061	0.9289
Executive	−0.0322	0.2854	0.9102
Tactical Operations			
Intelligence	0.0268	0.0634	0.6729
Engineering/Maintenance	−0.2208	0.0364	0.0001
Administration	−0.1002	0.0420	0.0169
Supply/Procurement	0.0514	0.0566	0.3638
Nonoccupational	0.4587	0.2783	0.0993
Cohort 77			
Cohort 80	−0.3222	0.0283	0.0001
	Retained	Count	
	Yes	16176	
	No	8852	

Table C.16

Retained During O-4
(Control for officer's entry path)

Variable	Parameter Estimate	Standard Error	Pr > Chi-Square
Intercept	3.0720	0.1006	0.0001
Prior Service	−1.6492	0.0641	0.0001
Army			
Navy	−0.5800	0.0766	0.0001
Marines	−0.0018	0.1095	0.9867
Air Force	0.0268	0.0721	0.7098
Academy			
ROTC Scholarship	0.3504	0.1197	0.0034
ROTC Regular	0.5998	0.1099	0.0001
OCS/OTS	−0.0937	0.0996	0.3468
Direct Appointment	−0.0687	0.1886	0.7156
Unknown Accession	−0.3149	0.1115	0.0047
White Male			
Black Male	−0.3291	0.1272	0.0097
Other Male	0.5357	0.3290	0.1035
White Female	0.3154	0.1751	0.0717
Black Female	0.6101	0.6283	0.3316
Other Female	−0.6941	0.7992	0.3852
Executive	0.1708	0.3363	0.6116
Tactical Operations			
Intelligence	−0.0105	0.1486	0.9437
Engineering/Maintenance	−0.2072	0.0809	0.0104
Administration	−0.4251	0.0948	0.0001
Supply/Procurement	0.1531	0.1222	0.2103
Cohort 67			
Cohort 70	−0.1664	0.0770	0.0307
Cohort 77	−0.5086	0.0677	0.0001
	Retained	Count	
	Yes	15682	
	No	1874	

Table C.17

Retained During O-5
(Control for officer's entry path)

Variable	Parameter Estimate	Standard Error	Pr > Chi-Square
Intercept	0.6942	0.0844	0.0001
Prior Service	−0.3760	0.0707	0.0001
Army			
Navy	1.0537	0.0793	0.0001
Marines	0.4959	0.1006	0.0001
Air Force	0.5555	0.0598	0.0001
Academy			
ROTC Scholarship	−0.0411	0.1084	0.7047
ROTC Regular	−0.2017	0.0847	0.0172
OCS/OTS	−0.3453	0.0863	0.0001
Direct Appointment	−0.0982	0.1780	0.5812
Unknown Accession	−0.2154	0.1004	0.0319
White Male			
Black Male	0.4918	0.1650	0.0029
White Female	−0.2018	0.1872	0.2810
Black Female	0.0268	1.2300	0.9826
Executive	−0.3023	0.2870	0.2923
Tactical Operations			
Intelligence	−0.0325	0.1441	0.8214
Engineering/Maintenance	−0.1634	0.0883	0.0643
Administration	−0.0226	0.1075	0.8334
Supply/Procurement	0.0888	0.1218	0.4661
Cohort 67			
Cohort 70	−0.1318	0.0575	0.0220
Cohort 77			
	Retained	Count	
	Yes	5800	
	No	2665	

Table C.18

Retained During O-2
(Do not control for officer's entry path)

Variable	Parameter Estimate	Standard Error	Pr > Chi-Square
Intercept	2.0354	0.0375	0.0001
Army			
Navy	1.7200	0.0525	0.0001
Marines	−0.7276	0.0383	0.0001
Air Force	2.6058	0.0653	0.0001
Academy			
White Male			
Black Male	−0.1684	0.0605	0.0054
Other Male	−0.0023	0.1090	0.9833
White Female	−0.5248	0.0509	0.0001
Black Female	−0.5855	0.1099	0.0001
Other Female	−0.6814	0.2546	0.0074
Tactical Operations			
Cohort 77			
Cohort 80	0.2069	0.0486	0.0001
Cohort 83	−0.0836	0.0453	0.0648
Cohort 87	−0.7103	0.0443	0.0001
	Retained	Count	
	Yes	56926	
	No	4911	

Table C.19

Retained During O-3
(Do not control for officer's entry path)

Variable	Parameter Estimate	Standard Error	Pr > Chi-Square
Intercept	0.8007	0.0287	0.0001
Army			
Navy	−0.1915	0.0360	0.0001
Marines	−0.1046	0.0556	0.0598
Air Force	0.0459	0.0323	0.1554
Academy			
White Male			
Black Male	0.3756	0.0630	0.0001
Other Male	−0.0061	0.0955	0.9489
White Female	−0.3141	0.0462	0.0001
Black Female	0.2880	0.1267	0.0231
Other Female	−0.0118	0.3031	0.9689
Tactical Operations			
Cohort 77			
Cohort 80	−0.2748	0.0271	0.0001

	Retained	Count	
	Yes	16176	
	No	8852	

Table C.20

Retained During O-4
(Do not control for officer's entry path)

Variable	Parameter Estimate	Standard Error	Pr > Chi-Square
Intercept	2.3274	0.0584	0.0001
Army			
Navy	−1.0041	0.0635	0.0001
Marines	−0.1342	0.1015	0.1863
Air Force	0.2536	0.0650	0.0001
Academy			
White Male			
Black Male	−0.3336	0.1190	0.0051
Other Male	0.5966	0.3149	0.0582
White Female	0.4526	0.1623	0.0053
Black Female	0.6605	0.6006	0.2715
Other Female	−0.3985	0.7745	0.6069
Tactical Operations			
Cohort 67			
Cohort 70	0.1559	0.0643	0.0152
Cohort 77	−0.2087	0.0604	0.0006
	Retained	Count	
	Yes	15686	
	No	1875	

Table C.21

Retained During O-5
(Do not control for officer's entry path)

Variable	Parameter Estimate	Standard Error	Pr > Chi-Square
Intercept	0.3702	0.0438	0.0001
Army			
Navy	1.0418	0.0755	0.0001
Marines	0.4510	0.0964	0.0001
Air Force	0.5618	0.0534	0.0001
Academy			
White Male			
Black Male	0.4535	0.1643	0.0058
White Female	−0.2396	0.1813	0.1862
Black Female	0.0010	1.2354	0.9993
Tactical Operations			
Cohort 67			
Cohort 70	−0.0417	0.0478	0.3831
Cohort 77			

	Retained	Count
	Yes	5800
	No	2666

QUALITATIVE RESEARCH METHODOLOGY

Our qualitative research effort was designed to identify relevant perspectives on minority and gender differences in career development from three key groups of actors in the career-management system. The first group was those who actively manage or set policies regarding officer careers. The second key group included those who are asked to judge officer careers through the promotion board process. The third group was midcareer officers themselves. These three groups were identified to provide perspectives on how the career-management system is designed to work, how it actually works, and how it is perceived to work. In total, we interviewed 233 individuals across the four services. All discussions were held during the summer and fall of 1995. In this appendix we detail how individuals in each of these groups were selected to participate in our study, how we conducted our interviews, and what topics were covered.

INTERVIEWS WITH CAREER MANAGERS

We interviewed individuals from all four services who managed the various components of commissioned officer careers, including accessions, duty assignments, professional military education (PME) and graduate education, performance reviews, and selection boards. The objective of these interviews was to assess the formal career process and formalized policies and procedures affecting commissioned officer careers.

Selection of Participants

Each service provided us with a point of contact (POC) who assisted in identifying appropriate individuals with responsibility for planning, managing, or administering key career processes for commissioned officers. We instructed the service POC that we wanted to meet with individuals who could provide information on policies and procedures relating to: accessions, initial basic officer training, duty assignments, continuing officer education, promotion boards, augmentation boards, and command boards. We asked to interview one or two individuals for each area as the POC saw necessary to get a good overview of relevant policies and procedures.

Interview Format

The interviews were exploratory and unstructured in nature. In all, 30 interviews were conducted with some 40–45 officers and civilians. In order to foster an environment conducive to an open discussion of sensitive issues, participants were offered confidentiality regarding attribution of their comments. Further, no conversations were electronically recorded. Two or more RAND researchers participated in each interview, with one researcher conducting the interview and the other(s) taking notes. Notes from the interviews were combined with official and unofficial documentation, including: formal career guides, performance review materials and instructions, promotion board precepts, materials used to train promotion board members, and guidance to supervisors regarding how to write performance evaluations.

In addition, we participated in briefings and exercises designed to provide detailed information on the promotion board process. The Department of the Army Secretariat for Selection Boards conducted a mock promotion board using RAND researchers as board members. We were given an abbreviated version of the training that is given to actual board members and were then asked to evaluate a set of actual promotion candidate files. Our judgments were then compared to the outcomes from the actual promotion board.

FOCUS GROUPS WITH RECENT PROMOTION BOARD MEMBERS

We conducted eight focus groups (group interviews) with officers who had recently sat on either an O-5 or O-6 promotion board. We interviewed promotion board members both to explore their role as a "gatekeepers" for continued service and career progression of officers and to gather their broader reflections as senior officers who have reviewed a substantial number of officer career records. We centered our discussions on three issues: the functional process by which boards deliberate, the influence that a candidate's race or gender might have on deliberations, and the patterns of race and gender differences in career development that can be seen in promotion candidate files.

Selection of Participants

Each service provided a POC who identified officers who had sat on an O-5 or O-6 promotion board for line or line-restricted officers within the past 2–3 years. The POC and the appropriate Secretariat selected the officers to participate in our discussions based on guidelines provided by RAND. We requested that each service set up two separate groups for our discussions, one for those who had sat on an O-5 board and one for those who had sat on an O-6 board.

We requested that the group of participants be representative of actual boards, with an appropriate mix of occupations, minority status, or any other characteristics considered when boards are constituted. Due to the small number of women and minority officers at the O-6 and flag officer grades, we have chosen not to provide a detailed table on the background characteristics of the participants in these discussions, in order to preserve their confidentiality. However, the services, by and large, selected officers for our discussions with varied occupational, minority/ethnic, and gender characteristics. We requested that each group contain 6 to 8 participants. In total, we interviewed 45 officers through 8 separate focus groups.

Interview Format

The focus groups were conducted in a semistructured manner. Specific protocols were developed, but we allowed discussions to deviate considerably from the protocol when they took an informative turn. The protocol is reproduced in Appendix E.

In order to foster an open discussion, participants were offered confidentiality with RAND regarding the attribution of comments. Participants were also asked to respect the confidentiality of the other participants. No sessions were electronically taped. The interview team consisted of three researchers: a primary discussion leader, a secondary discussion leader, and a dedicated note taker. The note taker's responsibility was to record as much as possible of the actual dialog. These notes served as abbreviated transcripts of the discussions.

Board members must take an oath to keep board deliberations confidential. They are only permitted to discuss their deliberations with a representative of the Secretary of their service.[1] Therefore, the services had some concern with permitting RAND to conduct discussions with former promotion board members. RAND carefully devised its protocol to avoid conflict with this oath by not asking board members to discuss any particular board's deliberations or specific candidate's review. Certain services required that a service representative be present during the discussions to advise participants on what could and could not be discussed under the board's confidentiality oath. These service representatives agreed to the condition that the discussions were to be kept confidential with RAND and that they were not to report the statements made by individuals during the discussions. The board's confidentiality oath and the presence in some sessions of a service representative may certainly have inhibited some participants from speaking freely about the effect of a candidate's race or gender in board deliberations. However, we found most participants ready to engage in free and open expression of a broad diversity of opinions on the matters dis-

---

[1]This might occur in the case of an investigation into unusual outcomes or significant problems with the administration or conduct of the board on which they served. No one reported to us that this had occurred with his or her board.

cussed. The discussions were quite lively with participants actively challenging the judgments of others in the group.

FOCUS GROUPS AND INTERVIEWS WITH MIDCAREER OFFICERS

The third component of our qualitative research effort was an extensive series of one-on-one interviews and focus groups with midcareer commissioned officers, primarily officers at the O-3 and O-4 levels. The purpose of these interviews and focus groups was to compare actual experiences and perceptions of the career-management system with formal policies, structures, and processes. The one-on-one interviews were designed to document the careers of individual officers. We asked interviewees about their assignment histories, perceived performance and evaluation, other relevant career experiences and milestones, career goals, peer and mentoring relationships, and perceptions of the equal opportunity environment in their service. The focus groups addressed a similar set of issues, but in more general terms. In particular, the focus groups explored perceptions of a group's experiences contrasted to the experience of other groups, where the groups were defined around occupational, educational, minority and gender lines.

Selection of Participants

RAND worked with service POCs to identify a site in each service at which we could conduct our focus groups. An important consideration in selecting the sites was to ensure the availability of an adequate number of female and black officers for our discussions. Few sites had sufficient numbers in minority groups other than blacks for focus groups. Therefore, we limited the focus groups to white and black, male and female officers. Other minority officers were interviewed individually, except as noted below. We wanted to meet with white and black commissioned officers of both genders at the O-3 and O-4 level who were diverse according to accession source and branch, community, or occupation within their service. For some services, finding an adequate concentration of female and black officers at a single site proved problematic. We added a second site visit for the Air Force in order to include officers from a fighter wing. Table D.1 presents the list of selected sites

Table D.1

Sites Where Midcareer Officer Interviews and Focus Groups Were Held

Service	Location
Marine Corps	Camp Pendleton, Oceanside, California
Army	Fort Leavenworth, Leavenworth, Kansas
Air Force	Little Rock AFB, Little Rock, Arkansas
	Mountain Home AFB, Mountain Home, Idaho
Navy	San Diego Naval Base, San Diego, California

At each base, we worked with a POC to identify a sample of officers for our discussions. We requested a sample with equal numbers of white males, black males, white females, and black females. It was not always possible for a POC to identify our requested number of black officers. When this occurred, we agreed to substitute officers from other minority groups (primarily Hispanic officers). This happened in only a couple of instances. In total, we interviewed 143 midcareer officers either one on one or as part of a focus group. Table D.2 provides the racial and gender breakdown of these officers.

Within each of these racial/gender groups, we specified that the group be mixed by accession source and occupation as well. The group was to have participants who had attended the service academies, ROTC scholarship and nonscholarship, and OTS/OCS. In the Army and Marine Corps, the group was to have participants from Combat Arms (heavy and light), Combat Support, and Combat Service Support communities. In the Air Force, the group was to have participants from rated, operations support, mission support,

Table D.2

Race and Gender Composition of Midcareer Officers Interviewed

Service	Number	Percent
White Male	41	29%
Black Male	39	27%
White Female	41	29%
Black Female	22	15%

and Commander's staff assignments. In the Navy the group was to have participants from the surface, submarine, and air communities. Given restrictions on women's assignments, it was not always possible to select a group of women from each of these occupational or assignment groups. By and large, our sample at each site met the distribution requirements we specified.

Because the participants for these discussions were not drawn randomly, there may be a number of undesirable selection biases in our sample. First, the base staff could have stacked our sample with those who might offer opinions casting the military in a more positive light. A substantial bias from the POC stacking our sample is unlikely for a couple of reasons. POCs often struggled to meet our requirements for diversity according to accession source and occupation, thereby limiting their opportunity to stack the sample. Further, because there is often only a small number of women and black officers at any single location, we often ended up interviewing the majority of these officers available during our time on base. Finally, a substantial diversity of opinions was expressed during all of our discussions.

A second type of bias might have influenced our interviews. Those that participated in our discussions could have been those most interested in issues of racial or gender equity. Participation in our discussions was voluntary; officers who did not wish to participate could have made themselves unavailable for our discussions. It is hard for us to evaluate the degree to which this bias exists; yet a couple of factors are worth noting. First, a number of participants had limited knowledge about the purpose of our discussions. Second, participant responses varied considerably, from vehement support for one position or another to no strong opinions on any questions.

Interview Format

Both the one-on-one interviews and focus groups were semistructured. Separate protocols were developed for each and are reproduced in appendices F and G, respectively. Yet we allowed discussions to deviate considerably from the protocol when they took an informative turn. One-on-one interviews generally lasted about an hour; focus groups generally lasted one and one-half to two hours.

As in the other discussions, we offered participants confidentiality regarding attribution of comments. Focus group participants were asked to respect the confidentiality of other participants. No service representatives were present during any interviews or focus groups. No sessions were electronically recorded. A single interviewer generally conducted one-on-one interviews. The interviewer was responsible for producing written notes on the discussion. The focus group interview teams consisted of three researchers: a primary interviewer, a secondary interviewer, and a dedicated note taker. The note taker's responsibility was to record as much as possible of the actual dialog. These notes served as abbreviated transcripts of the discussions.

At each site, four separate focus groups were conducted: one for black males, one for white males, one for black females, and one for white females. The interview teams were mixed along both racial and gender lines and had substantial diversity with regard to academic discipline, military research experience, and personal military service. As stated in the text of the report, it was not possible for us to always match the race/gender of a focus group discussion leader to that of the discussion group's participants. This might have biased our data toward an understatement of perceived racial differences, as prior studies have shown that in responding to a white interviewer, blacks tend to underplay expressions of racial differences in experiences or attitudes (see Anderson et al., 1988; Davis, 1977). Similar behavior is expected with white responses to a black interviewer (Hatchett and Schuman, 1975–76). However, we do not feel that our inability to consistently match interviewer and interviewee characteristics substantially limited the quality of our discussions. In fact, we sometimes found that discussion group leaders of similar racial/gender characteristics were less productive at eliciting rich discussions. Some participants appeared to "assume" that interviewers with similar background characteristics held a more personal understanding of that group's situation and consequently provided less detail about their experiences and perceptions.

PROMOTION BOARD MEMBER FOCUS GROUP PROTOCOL

I. INTRODUCTION

First, I'd like to introduce myself and my colleagues. . . .

Q1:   Have you been told anything about why you are here today?

As you probably know, we are from RAND. RAND is a nonprofit research organization that serves as a federally funded research and development center of OSD, the Air Force, and the Army. As part of our work for OSD, we are studying the accession and career progression of minority and female officers. This research is supporting an officer pipeline study being conducted by the Under Secretary of Defense for Personnel and Readiness at the request of Mr. Perry. Our study team has already talked to the headquarters offices responsible for officer management policy in all the services. We are also interviewing midcareer officers to get their views. Our purpose in talking to you today is to further refine our understanding of how promotion boards operate and what steps an officer must take to be competitive for promotion to O-5 and O-6. We would appreciate your feedback if we miss any important issues or spend too much time on unimportant ones.

Your participation in this discussion is entirely voluntary. If you do not wish to participate, you may leave. Also, please feel free to not answer any questions that you are uncomfortable with. We understand your legal obligation not to discuss the specific deliberations of the promotion boards you have sat on. We have tried to focus our questions on the general processes and judgments you have made and avoid matters that should remain confidential. If you feel that answering any of our questions would violate your oath as a former board member, just let us know and we will move on to another question.

We will keep everything you say confidential. We will not keep a list of your names. (X) will be taking notes during our discussion, but will not insert any names into the notes. We will not show the notes to anyone outside of RAND. Our report will include only a general description of the people who participated from all the services and a summary of the discussions from which the identity and views of the participants cannot be inferred. We also ask each of you to commit to keeping today's discussion confidential. What each of you says should remain in this room.

If there are any issues you prefer to discuss with us privately, you should feel free to call any of us at the number listed on our business card.

Q2:   Before we get started, do you have any questions about us, RAND, or the purpose of this discussion or project?

Q3:   *Please introduce yourself and tell us briefly about your military background and the number and types of selection boards you have served on.*

II. PROMOTION BOARD MEMBERSHIP

A. Board selection and composition

Q1:   *Basics: size*

Q2:   *Who appoints*

Q3:   *Eligibility requirements*

Q4:   *How selected*

Q5:   *What balance is sought*

Q6:   *Why were you chosen to serve*

Q7:   *Can you serve multiple times*

B. Training

Q1:   *What type of formal/informal training*

Q2:   *Was it adequate*

Q3:   *What is the most important thing to know*

Q4:   *Did sense of who gets promoted change*

C. Mandate

Q1:   *How much detail on what the group you promote should look like: occupation, branch, race, gender, joint service*

III. PROCESS OF FILE DELIBERATION

A. Logistics

Q1:   *How often do boards meet and for how long*

Q2:   *Meet as a whole or in subgroups*

B. Process

1.   File presentation

Q1:   *How is file presented, how much time*

Q2:   *Role of presenter: advocate for whom*

Q3:   *Time on each case, variation in time*

Q4:   *What does discussion sound like*

Q5:   *Do some members hold greater sway in discussions*

2.   File scoring

Q1: *At what stage are files scored, how is scoring done*

Q2: *What kind of score: absolute, relative*

3. Final tallying, revision and submission

Q1: Who summarizes results, who sees the summary

Q2: How tallied, by what groups

Q3: Are scores ever changed

4. Checks and balances

Q1: What prevents an individual from unfairly scoring a group

Q2: Are ratings of individual board members tallied

Q3: Check on consistency of scores

Q4: Any computer models used

Q5: Other factors which might prompt the review of a file

IV. THE SUBSTANCE OF FILE DELIBERATION

A. Composition of file

Q1: What actually is in the file and how is it laid out

B. Sorting the wheat from the chaff

Q1: How do you approach getting information from a file

Q2: What does the picture tell you

Q3: Do you read OER's, how carefully, and what parts

Q4: Does it matter who wrote the OER

C. Decisionmaking algorithms

Q1: What formulas guide your decisionmaking

Q2: What career steps must an individual have accomplished

Q3: What boxes to O-4, to O-5, which are essential

Q4: How important is one's career field to the evaluation

Q5: Is it hard to judge candidates from other career fields

Q6:   How important is post-graduate education

Q7:   How important is service school attendance

Q8:   How important is HQ assignment, command experience, joint service assignment

Q9:   Is the timing of these experiences important

Q10:   How important are signs of willingness to move

Q11:   How do background and demographic characteristics play

Q12:   What are the negative signs looked for: disciplinary infractions, drinking/drug problem, weight standard

Q13:   What is the time frame for evaluating performance

Q14:   How is an individual's history evaluated: overcome disadvantage, points for improvement

Q15:   What makes one eligible for below-the-zone (BTZ) promotion

Q16:   Does one BTZ promotion increase/decrease chance for future BTZ promotions

Q17:   What characterizes those who will not make promotion

Q18:   Is an officer aware of all items in his/her file

Q19:   How is all the information weighed, what takes precedence

Q20:   How formulaic is this, would two boards reach same answer

V. IMPACT OF RACE/GENDER

A. Board selection and composition

Q1:   Is race/gender a factor in selection for board

B. Training

Q1:   Did the formal/informal training focus directly on any issues related to race/gender

C. Tallying and revising scores

Q1:   Did the results from your board get tallied by race/gender for you to consider

Q2:   Are the files reconsidered as a function of race/gender

D. Evaluating a file

Q1:   Were you aware of the race/gender of the person you were evaluating

Q2:   Can you think of advantages/disadvantages that minorities/women may have in checking off the boxes

Q3:   Are there other ways which might make it difficult for women/minorities to be "good officers," which might lead to poorer performance or evaluations

Q4:   Are there advantages conferred on minorities/women by virtue of their status

Q5:   Given two equally qualified candidates, one white/male and one nonwhite/female, is one more likely to be given a leg up than the other

MIDCAREER OFFICER ONE-ON-ONE INTERVIEW PROTOCOL

I. INTRODUCTION

First, I'd like to introduce myself. My name is . . . , I am a (insert your favorite disciplinary association here) with the RAND Corporation. RAND is a nonprofit research organization that serves as a federally funded research and development center of OSD, the Air Force, and the Army.

Q1: Have you been told anything about why you are here today?

As part of our work for OSD, we are studying the accession and career progression of minority and female officers. This research is supporting an officer pipeline study being conducted by the Under Secretary of Defense for Personnel and Readiness at the request of Mr. Perry. Our study team has already talked to the headquarters offices responsible for officer management policy in all the services. We are also interviewing officers who have sat on promotion boards to get their views.

Our purpose in talking to you today is to further develop our understanding of the development of officer careers and to get your views on what steps an officer must take to be competitive for promotion to O-5 and O-6. I'm going to be asking you a series of questions about training, assignments, milestones, evaluations, and so forth. While I'll occasionally ask questions directed at eliciting straightforward pieces of information about your career, most of my questions will try to elicit your opinions and observations of how the process works.

Your participation in this discussion is entirely voluntary. If you do not wish to participate, you may leave. Also, please feel free to not answer any questions that you are uncomfortable with. We will keep everything you say confidential. We will not keep a list of your names. I will take notes during our discussion, but I will not insert your name into the notes. The notes will not be shown to anyone outside of RAND. Our report will include only a general description of the people who participated from all the services and a summary of the discussions from which the identity and views of the participants cannot be inferred.

Q2: *Before we get started, do you have any [further] questions about us, RAND, or the purpose of this discussion or project?*

Q3: *Please tell me the basic information about your current position: Rank, YOS, Occupation, Commission Source*

Q4: *Tell me also about your civilian educational background: degrees, majors, schools*

II. BACKGROUND

A. Current information

Q1: *Rank, YOS, Occupation, Commission Source*

B. Other background information

Q1: Civilian Education: degrees, majors and schools

III. BECOMING AN OFFICER (10)

A. Motivations

Q1: *How did you come to be an officer: circumstances and motivations*

Q2: *Are you from a military family*

Q3: *Did you intend to serve for a career, or get out when finished your initial enlistment*

B. Accession

Q1:   Did you have a particular career field in mind when you joined

Q2:   Did you know what your career field would be when you joined

Q3:   How well prepared for military service were you

Q4:   Did you think you have received advantages/disadvantages due to your commission source

IV. FIRST YEARS (15)

A. OCS/OTS/TBS

Q1:   What was XXX like for you: particular successes/difficulties

Q2:   How well did you do in XXX

Q3:   Did you know others who had difficulty getting through XXX? What kind of difficulties

B. Occupational choice

Q1:   How did you choose your occupation

Q2:   Is the occupation you received the one you wanted

Q3:   Did you get any advice on which occupations were the best to choose

C. First duty assignment

Q1:   What was your first duty assignment

Q2:   Was it the one you wanted, were you able to exert any influence in the assignment process

Q3:   Did you get advice on which assignments were best

Q4:   How did you do in your first assignment

Q5:   Do you consider this assignment to have been a good first assignment

D. Occupational schooling

Q1:   *When did you attend your first occupational school*

Q2:   *Did you have any difficulty during the program, how did you do in the program*

Q3:   *Did you know others who had difficulties, what type of difficulties*

E. Remaining assignments in first couple of years

Q1:   *What was the next assignment you had after. . . .*

Q2:   *How did you get this assignment*

Q3:   *How did you do in this assignment*

Q4:   *Do you believe that this was a good assignment to have*

Q5:   *During this period did you receive any promotions or get augmented: Was this ahead of your peers, on par with your peers, behind your peers*

F. Mentors

Q1:   *Were there individuals whom you would consider to have acted as mentor during these early years?*

Q2:   *What did they provide: information, access, influence*

G. Finding stride

Q1:   *How hard was it for you to find your stride as an officer: hit the ground running or slow starter*

Q2:   *When you look back on this period, how did being a woman/minority color your experience: preparedness, cultural dissonance, peer relationships, supervisory relationships*

V. BEYOND INITIAL OBLIGATION

A. Decision

Q1:   When did you decide to continue on beyond your initial obligation

Q2:   To what extent did this decision reflect an assessment of your chances to remain until retirement

B. Assignments

Q1:   What kind of assignments did you have in this intermediate period: command responsibilities, joint duty

Q2:   How much of a say did you have in which assignments you received

Q3:   What drove your choice of assignments

C. Performance reviews

Q1:   Have your performance reviews accurately reflected your performance

Q2:   How would you characterize your performance reviews

Q3:   Have you ever felt that you were being judged on more than your competence on the job, were there any situations where race/gender appeared to affect your evaluation (negative/positive)

D. Schooling

Q1:   What type of schooling have you completed: residence or correspondence

Q2:   Did you have any difficulties completing these courses

E. Augmentation

Q1:   When did you apply for/receive augmentation, was this early/late/on time with your peers

F. Promotions

Q1: *When did you receive promotions during this period, were any promotions above or below zone*

Q2: *Have you been passed over for any promotions*

G. Mentors

Q1: *Were there individuals whom you would consider to have acted as mentor during these intermediate years?*

Q2: *What did they provide: information, access, influence*

Q3: *How was their mentoring different than mentors you had in your early years*

VI. O-5 AND BEYOND

A. Intentions

Q1: *Are you interested in attaining rank of LTC/COL/GEN, What do you think your chances are*

B. Career management

Q1: *What are you doing to insure that you will be competitive for promotion*

Q2: *What assignment would you like to receive next*

Q3: *To what degree have you/can you consciously managed your career*

Q4: *How did you know what would be good career moves*

C. Model officer

Q1: *What does the model officer look like: social/cultural background, economic background, educational background, military family tradition, source of commission, occupation, marital status, interests and hobbies, tastes in music/art/fashion.*

Q2:   To what degree have you conformed to this image or diverged from it

Q3:   Has this helped/hurt your career

VII. RACE AND GENDER ISSUES

A. Incidents

Q1:   Do you find yourself/others guarded in interactions with officers of different race/gender: what types of situations, how does it affect interactions

Q2:   Have you ever been in a situation where a misunderstanding or misperception arose due to your or another's race/gender, how was it resolved

Q3:   Have there been any situations with those under your command where a misunderstanding/misperception arose. . . . How did the situation get resolved

Q4:   Have you observed any situations in other settings. . . .

B. Effect on career

Q1:   Do you feel that your race/gender has affected any aspects of your career to date, the next stages of your career: decisions made, paths pursued, guidance received, ratings received

C. Does race/gender still matter?

Q1:   Does race/gender still matter? Justify your answer in light of the observed differences in promotion and separation

MIDCAREER OFFICER FOCUS GROUP PROTOCOL

I. INTRODUCTION

First, I'd like to introduce myself and my colleague . . .

Q1: Have you been told anything about why you are here today?

RAND is a nonprofit research organization that serves as a federally funded research and development center of OSD, the Air Force, and the Army. As part of our work for OSD, we are studying the accession and career progression of minority and female officers. This research is supporting an officer pipeline study being conducted by the Under Secretary of Defense for Personnel and Readiness at the request of Mr. Perry. Our study team has already talked to the headquarters offices responsible for officer management policy in all the services. We are also interviewing officers who have sat on promotion boards to get their views.

Our purpose in talking to you today is to further develop our understanding of the development of officer careers and to get your views on what steps an officer must take to be competitive for promotion to O-5 and O-6. We're going to be asking you a series of questions about training, assignments, milestones, evaluations, and so forth. While we'll occasionally ask questions directed at eliciting straightforward pieces of information, most of our questions will try to elicit your opinions and observations of how the process works.

Your participation in this discussion is entirely voluntary. If you do not wish to participate, you may leave. Also, please feel free to not answer any questions that you are uncomfortable with. We will keep everything you say confidential. We will not keep a list of your names. (X) will be taking notes during our discussion, but will not insert your name into the notes. We will not show the notes to any-one outside of RAND. Our report will include only a general descrip-tion of the people who participated from all the services and a sum-mary of the discussions from which the identity and views of the participants cannot be inferred. We also ask each of you to commit to keeping today's discussion confidential. What each of you says should remain in this room.

At the end of our discussion, we will pass out a very short evaluation form. If there are any issues you prefer to discuss with us privately, you can indicate on the form how we can contact you. You should also feel free to call any of us at the number listed on our business card.

Q2:   *Before we get started, do you have any [further] questions about us, RAND, or the purpose of this discussion or project?*

Q3:   *Please introduce yourself and tell us briefly about your back-ground: college, accession source, rank, occupation/branch and years of service*

II. BECOMING AN OFFICER (10)

A. Motivations

Q1:   *Why do people choose to become officers*

Q2:   *What choices and actions signal career intentions*

Q3:   *Do motivations affect career-related decisions*

B. Accessions

Q1:   *What influence does source of commission have*

Q2:   *Are officers from different commission sources equally prepared for their career*

III. FIRST YEARS (15)

A. Failures

Q1: *What reasons are there for separation in first year or two: problems in basic school, lack of fit*

Q2: *What might explain race/gender differences in separation rates during this period*

B. Key Events

1. Choice of Occupation

Q1: *What factors affect an individual's choice of occupation*

Q2: *Does occupational choice affect later career chances*

Q3: *Are individuals aware of this when they make choice*

Q4: *How does an officer learn this and influence the assignment*

Q5: *Are there occupations minorities/women are more likely to choose*

2. First Assignment

Q1: *How much does one's first assignment matter*

Q2: *Are there good/bad assignments*

Q3: *How does an officer learn this*

Q4: *How does an officer influence the assignment*

IV. BEYOND INITIAL OBLIGATION (15)

A. Decision

Q1: *Why are some more likely than others to leave after their initial obligation*

Q2: *What internal/external pressures act on women at this time*

Q3: *What's the constancy of intentions from time of accession*

B. Ticket punches

Q1:   *In the 4–6 years period, what experiences are officers trying to get: command, school, early augmentation*

Q2:   *What assignments are considered good/bad*

Q3:   *How does one learn about the tickets to punch and influence the ability to get them punched*

C. Mentors

Q1:   *How important to have a mentor in first 6–7 years*

Q2:   *Who has/doesn't have mentors, why*

Q3:   *What do mentors provide: information, access, influence*

V. 0-5 AND BEYOND

A. Ideal career track

Q1:   *What does the ideal career track look like: assignments, commands, school attendance, timing of these factors*

Q2:   *Other "hidden" requirements?*

Q3:   *How do you get information on the ideal career track*

Q4:   *How do you influence the ability to fill boxes*

B. Who makes it /who doesn't make it

Q1:   *Why might someone choose not to pursue the O-5–O-6 rank*

Q2:   *How easy to juggle career and family*

Q3:   *How early in a career can you identify those who will be COL v. those who won't make LTC*

Q4:   *What particular factors might directly affect women and minorities at this stage*

VI. EVALUATIONS AND BOARDS

A. OERs

Q1: *Beyond job performance, how can an officer work to get best possible evaluation: personal relationship w/supervisor, background, interests, tastes, cultural, geographic*

Q2: *How do perceptions/misunderstandings due to race/gender affect evaluation*

Q3: *What other than job performance affects one's reputation as an officer: social, volunteer, sports/hobbies, spouse*

Q4: *Does race/gender affect perceptions and expectations in these areas, positive/negative*

Q5: *Other important informal rules, in what career segments*

B. File

Q1: *What can officer do to ensure file is accurate*

Q2: *How proactive are officers in doing this*

C. Perception of board deliberations

Q1: *Does race/gender affect promotion chances or chances before other boards*

VII. RACE AND GENDER ISSUES

A. Social relations

Q1: *Is there social self-segregation*

B. Misunderstanding/expectations

Q1: *Do misunderstandings arise*

Q2: *Are their perceptions or expectations that lead the misunderstandings to arise*

Q3: *Have issues related to sexual/racial harassment affected interactions between males and females*

Q4:   Does the fear of sexual/racial harassment influence choices made by individuals regarding their military career

C. Superiors' comfort with race/gender

Q1:   Are some superiors/senior rates more comfortable with individuals of a different race and gender

D. Assignments and requirements

Q1:   Are some assignment environments more comfortable for those of a different race and gender

Q2:   Do some educational/technical requirements and assignments affect perceptions of a person's authority on the basis of race/gender

E. Does race/gender still matter?

Q1:   Does race/gender still matter? Justify your answer in light of the observed differences in promotion and separation

REFERENCES

Air Force Inspector General, *The Inspector General of the Air Force Special Management Review: Sexual Harassment in the Active Duty Force and Air Reserve Components*, Washington, D.C.: Government Printing Office, June 1993, as abstracted in GAO/NSIAD-95-103.

Anderson, Barbara A., Brian D. Silver, and Paul R. Abramson, "The Effects of the Race of the Interviewer on Race-Related Attitudes of Black Respondents in SRC/CPS National Election Studies," *Public Opinion Quarterly*, Vol. 52, 1988, pp. 289–324.

Asch, Beth J., M. Rebecca Kilburn, and Jacob A. Klerman, *Attracting College Bound Youth Into the Military: Toward Developing New Recruiting Policy Options*, Santa Monica, CA: RAND, MR-984-OSD, 1999.

Bartol, K. M., "The Effect of Male Versus Female Leaders on Follower Satisfaction and Performance," *Journal of Business Research*, Vol. 3, 1975, pp. 33–42.

Bastian, Lisa D., Anita R. Lancaster, and Heidi E. Reyst, *Department of Defense 1995 Sexual Harassment Survey*, Washington, D.C.: Defense Manpower Data Center, 96-014, December 1996.

Bean, F. D., and M. Tienda, *The Hispanic Population of the United States (The Population of the United States in the 1980s)*, New York: Russell Sage Foundation, 1987.

Bielby, William T., and Denise D. Bielby, "I Will Follow Him: Family Ties, Gender-role Beliefs, and Reluctance to Relocate for a Better

Job," *American Journal of Sociology*, Vol. 97, March 1992, pp. 1241–1267.

Biernat, Monica, and Diane Kobrynowicz, "Gender- and Race-Based Standards of Competence: Lower Minimum Standards but Higher Ability Standards for Devalued Groups," *Journal of Personality and Social Psychology*, Vol. 72, No. 3, 1997, pp. 544–557.

Bobo, Lawrence, and James R. Kluegel, "Opposition to Race-Targeting: Self-Interest, Stratification Ideology, or Racial Attitudes?" *American Sociological Review*, Vol. 58, 1993, pp. 443–464.

Bowman, William R., "Do Engineers Make Better Naval Officers?" *Armed Forces and Society*, Vol. 16, No. 2, Winter 1990, pp. 271–286.

Cox, Taylor H., and Stella M. Nkomo, "A Race and Gender-Group Analysis of the Early Career Experience of MBAs," *Work and Occupations*, Vol. 18, No. 4, November 1991, pp. 431–446.

Culbertson, Amy L., Paul Rosenfeld, and Carol E. Newell, *Sexual Harassment in the Active-Duty Navy: Findings from the 1991 Navy-wide Survey*, Washington, D.C.: NPRDC, December 1993, as abstracted in GAO/NSIAD-95-103.

Cymrot, Donald J., with Kletus S. Lawler, *Qualification of Surface Warfare Officers*, Alexandria, VA: Center for Naval Analyses, CRM 89-316, April 1990.

Davis, Darren W., "The Direction of Race of Interviewer Effects Among African-Americans: Donning the Black Mask," *American Journal of Political Science*, Vol. 41, No. 1, January 1997, pp. 309–322.

Defense Manpower Data Center, *Data on 1992 DoD Surveys of Officers and Enlisted Personnel*, Washington, D.C., August 20, 1993.

Defense Manpower Data Center, *Defense Manpower Data Center Profile-2000*, Washington, D.C., 2000.

Department of Defense, Office of the Assistant Secretary of Defense (Force Management Policy), *Population Representation in the Military Services*, Washington, D.C., November 1996.

Department of Defense, Office of the Assistant Secretary of Defense (Personnel and Readiness), *Population Representation in the Military Services, Fiscal Year 1997*, Washington, D.C., November 1998.

Dovidio, J. F., and R. H. Fazio, "New Technologies for the Direct and Indirect Assessment of Attitudes," in Judith M. Tanur, ed., *Questions About Questions*, New York: Russell Sage Foundation, 1992.

Dreher, George F., and Taylor H. Cox, Jr., "Race, Gender, and Opportunity: A Study of Compensation Attainment and the Establishment of Mentoring Relationships," *Journal of Applied Psychology*, Vol. 81, No. 3, 1996, pp. 297–308.

Dreher, George F., and Ronald A. Ash, "A Comparative Study of Mentoring Among Men and Women in Managerial, Professional, and Technical Positions," *Journal of Applied Psychology*, Vol. 75, No. 5, 1990, pp. 539–546.

Ehrenberg, Ronald G., and Donna S. Rothstein, "Do Historically Black Institutions of Higher Education Confer Unique Advantages on Black Students? An Initial Analysis," in *Choices and Consequences: Contemporary Policy Issues*, Ithaca, NY: ILR Press, 1994, pp. 89–137.

Fagenson, E.A., "The Mentor Advantage: Perceived Career/Job Experiences of Proteges vs. Non-Proteges," *Journal of Organizational Behavior*, Vol. 10, 1989, pp. 309-320.

Feagin, Joe R., and Melvin P. Sikes, *Living with Racism: The Black Middle-Class Experience*, Boston, MA: Beacon Press, 1994.

Firestone, Juanita M., and Richard J. Harris, "Sexual Harassment in the U.S. Military: Individualized and Environmental Contexts," *Armed Forces and Society*, Vol. 21, No. 1, Fall 1994, pp. 25–43.

Fitzgerald, Louise F., Suzanne Swan, and Karla Fischer, "Why Didn't She Just Report Him? The Psychological and Legal Implications of

Women's Responses to Sexual Harassment," *Journal of Social Issues*, Vol. 51, No. 1, Spring 1995, pp. 117–138.

Frazier, Patricia A., Caroline C. Cochran, and Andrea M. Olson, "Social Science Research on Lay Definitions of Sexual Harassment," *Journal of Social Issues*, Vol. 51, No. 1, Spring 1995, pp. 21–37.

Gilroy, Curtis, Mark Eitelberg, John Enns, Susan Hosek, Rebecca Kilburn, Janice Laurence, Steven Mehay, Peter Tiemeyer, Naomi Verdugo, *Career Progression of Minority and Women Officers*, Office of the Under Secretary of Defense (Personnel and Readiness), Washington, D.C., August 1999.

Goldin, Claudia, *Career and Family: College Women Look to the Past*, Cambridge, MA: National Bureau of Economic Research, Inc., Working Paper No. 5188, July 1995.

Greene, William H., *Econometric Analysis*, New York: Macmillan Publishing Company, 1993.

Gutek, B. A., and M. P. Koss, "Changed Women and Changed Organizations: Consequences of Coping with Sexual Harassment," *Journal of Vocational Behavior*, Vol. 43, 1993, p. 28.

Haccoun, D. M., R. Haccoun, and G. Salay, "Sex Differences in the Appropriateness of Supervisory Styles: A Nonmanagement View," *Journal of Applied Psychology*, Vol. 63, 1978, pp. 124–127.

Hallinan, Maureen T., "Classroom Racial Composition and Children's Friendships," *Social Forces*, Vol. 61, No. 1, September 1982, pp. 56–72.

Hamilton, David L., and Tina K. Trolier, "Stereotypes and Stereotyping: An Overview of the Cognitive Approach," in J. Dovidio and S. Gaertner, eds., *Prejudice, Discrimination, and Racism*, Orlando: Academic Press, 1986, pp. 127–163.

Hansen, P., *Sex Differences in Supervision*, American Psychological Association Convention, New Orleans, 1974.

Harrell, Margaret C., and Laura L. Miller, *New Opportunities for Military Women: Effects Upon Readiness, Cohesion and Morale*, Santa Monica, CA: RAND, MR-896-OSD, 1997.

Hatchett, S., and H. Schuman, "White Respondents and Race-of-Interviewer Effects," *Public Opinion Quarterly*, Vol. 39, 1975–76, pp. 523–528.

Hosek, James R., and Mark Totten, *Does Perstempo Hurt Reenlistment? The Effect of Long or Hostile Perstempo on Reenlistment*, Santa Monica, CA: RAND, MR-990-OSD, 1998.

Inman, Mary L., and Robert S. Baron, "Influence of Prototypes on Perceptions of Prejudice," *Journal of Personality and Social Psychology*, Vol. 70, No. 4, 1996, pp. 727–739.

Jones, Edward W., Jr., "Black Managers: The Dream Deferred," *Harvard Business Review*, May–June 1986, pp. 84–93.

Kanter, Rosabeth Moss, *Men and Women of the Corporation*, New York: Basic Books, 1977.

Kissam, E., et al., *Hispanic Response to Census Enumeration Forms and Procedures, Executive Summary*, submitted to Center for Survey Methods Research, Bureau of the Census, by Aguirre International, San Mateo, CA; Reference Task Order No. 46-YABC-2-0001, 1993.

Kluegel, James R., "Trends in Whites' Explanations of the Black-White Gap in Socioeconomic Status, 1977-1989," *American Sociological Review*, Vol. 55, 1990, pp. 512–525.

Kluegel, James R., and Eliot R. Smith, "Affirmative Action Attitudes: Effects of Self-Interest, Racial Affect, and Stratification Beliefs on Whites' Views," *Social Forces*, Vol. 61, No. 3, March 1983, pp. 797–824.

Kluegel, James R., and Eliot R. Smith, "Whites' Beliefs About Blacks' Opportunity," *American Sociological Review*, Vol. 47, 1982, pp. 518–532.

Kram, K. E., *Mentoring at Work: Developmental Relationships in Organizational Life*, Glenview, IL: Scott, Foresman, 1985.

Kravitz, David A., "Attitudes Toward Affirmative Action Plans Directed at Blacks: Effects of Plan and Individual Differences," *Journal of Applied Social Psychology*, Vol. 25, No. 24, 1995, pp. 2192–2220.

Kravitz, David A., and Judith Platania, "Attitudes and Beliefs About Affirmative Action: Effects of Target and of Respondent Sex and Ethnicity," *Journal of Applied Psychology*, Vol. 78, No. 6, 1993, pp. 928–938.

Marsden, Peter V., Arne L. Kalleberg, and Cynthia R. Cook, "Gender Differences in Organizational Commitment Influences of Work Positions and Family Roles," *Work and Occupations*, Vol. 20, No. 3, August 1993, pp. 368–390.

Martin, Patricia Yancey, Dianne Harrison, and Diana Dinitto, "Advancement for Women in Hierarchical Organizations: A Multilevel Analysis of Problems and Prospects," *The Journal of Applied Behavioral Science*, Vol. 19, No. 1, 1983, pp. 19–33.

Martindale, M., *Sexual Harassment in the Military: 1988*, Washington, D.C.: Defense Manpower Data Center, 1990.

Mehay, Stephen L., *Analysis of Performance Data for Junior Navy and Marine Corps Officers*, Monterey, CA: Naval Postgraduate School, October 1995.

Metz, Mary Haywood, *Different by Design: The Context and Character of Three Magnet Schools*, Madison: University of Wisconsin, Department of Educational Policy Studies, 1986.

Miles, M., and A. M. Huberman, *Qualitative Data Analysis*, Thousand Oaks, CA: Sage Publications, 1994.

Miller, Laura L., "Not Just Weapons of the Weak: Gender Harassment as a Form of Protest for Army Men," *Social Psychology Quarterly*, Vol. 60, No. 1, 1997, pp. 32–51.

Moskos, Charles C., and John Sibley Butler, *All That We Can Be: Black Leadership and Racial Integration the Army Way*, New York: Basic Books, 1996.

National Research Council, *Modernizing the U.S. Census*, Barry Edmonston and Charles Schultze, eds., Washington, D.C.: National Academy Press, 1995.

North, James H., Dan D. Goldhaber, with Kletus S. Lawler, and Jeremy N. Suess, *Successful Officer Careers: Analysis of Augmentation, Promotion, and Voluntary Continuation*, Alexandria, VA: Center for Naval Analyses, CRM 95-55, August 1995.

North, James H., and Karen D. Smith, *Officer Accession Characteristics and Success at Officer Candidate School, Commissioning, and The Basic School*, Alexandria, VA: Center for Naval Analyses, CRM 93-81.10, December 1993.

North, James H., Donald J. Cymrot, Karen D. Smith, Neil B. Carey, *Perspectives on Minority Officer Success Rates in the Marine Corps*, Alexandria, VA: Center for Naval Analyses, June 1994.

Nosworthy, Glenn J., James A. Lea, and R.C.L. Lindsay, "Opposition to Affirmative Action: Racial Affect and Traditional Value Predictors Across Four Programs," *Journal of Applied Social Psychology*, Vol. 25, No, 4, 1995, pp. 314–337.

Poskocil, Art, "Encounters Between Blacks and White Liberals: The Collision of Stereotypes," *Social Forces*, Vol. 55, No. 3, March 1977, pp. 715–727.

Rosen, B., and T. H. Jerdee, "The Influence of Sex-role Stereotypes on Evaluations of Male and Female Supervisory Behavior," *Journal of Applied Psychology*, Vol. 57, 1973, pp. 44–48.

Rostker, B., et al., *The Defense Officer Personnel Management Act of 1980: A Retrospective Assessment*, Santa Monica, CA: RAND, R-4246-FMP, 1993.

Rubin, H., and I. Rubin, *Qualitative Interviewing: The Art of Hearing Data*, Thousand Oaks, CA: Sage Publications, 1995.

Ruggiero, Karen M., and Donald M. Taylor, "Why Minority Group Members Perceive or Do Not Perceive the Discrimination That Confronts Them: The Role of Self-Esteem and Perceived Control," *Journal of Personality and Social Psychology*, Vol. 72, No. 2, 1997, pp. 373–389.

Saal, Frank E., and S. Craig Moore, "Perceptions of Promotion Fairness and Promotion Candidates' Qualifications," *Journal of Applied Psychology*, Vol. 78, No. 1, 1993, pp. 105–110.

Schein, V. E., "Sex Role Stereotyping, Ability and Performance: Prior Research and New Directions," *Personnel Psychology*, Vol. 31, 1978, pp. 259–267.

Secretary of the Army, *Senior Review Panel Report on Sexual Harassment*, Volume One, Washington, D.C., July 1997.

Secretary of the Army, *Senior Review Panel Report on Sexual Harassment*, Volume Two, Washington, D.C., July 1997.

Sherman, M. F., et al., "Racial and Gender Differences in Perceptions of Fairness: When Race Is Involved in a Job Promotion," *Perceptual and Motor Skills*, Vol. 57, 1983, pp. 719–728.

Steckler, Nicole A., and Robert Rosenthal, "Sex Differences in Nonverbal and Verbal Communication with Bosses, Peers and Subordinates," *Journal of Applied Psychology*, Vol. 70, No. 1, February 1985, pp. 157–163.

Steeh, Charolotte, Maria Krysan, "The Polls-Trends: Affirmative Action and the Public, 1970-1995," *Public Opinion Quarterly*, Vol. 60, 1996, pp. 128–158.

Thomas, David A., "Racial Dynamics in Cross-Race Development Relationships," *Administrative Science Quarterly*, Vol. 38, 1993, pp. 169–194.

Thomas, David A., "The Impact of Race on Managers' Experiences of Developmental Relationships (Mentoring and Sponsorship): An Intra-Organizational Study," *Journal of Organizational Behavior*, Vol. 11, 1990, pp. 479–492.

Tice, Jim, "Inner Sanctum," *Army Times*, Vol. 58, No. 5, September 1, 1997, p. 10.

Trempe, Johanne, André-Jean Rigny, and Robert R. Haccoun, "Subordinate Satisfaction with Male and Female Managers: Role of Perceived Supervisory Influence," *Journal of Applied Psychology*, Vol. 70, No. 1, 1985, pp. 44–47.

United States General Accounting Office, *Gender Issues: Analysis of Promotion and Career Opportunities Data*, Washington, D.C., GAO/NSIAD-98-157, May 1998.

United States General Accounting Office, *Military Equal Opportunity: Problems with Services' Complaint Systems Are Being Addressed by DoD*, Washington, D.C., GAO/NSIAD-96-9, January 1996.

United States General Accounting Office, *Military Equal Opportunity: Certain Trends in Racial and Gender Data May Warrant Further Analysis*, Washington, D.C., GAO/NSIAD-96-17, November 1995.

United States General Accounting Office, *Equal Opportunity: DoD Studies on Discrimination in the Military*, Washington, D.C., GAO/NSIAD-95-103, April 1995.

Whitley, Bernard E., Jr., Janet Ward Schofield, and Howard N. Snyder, "Peer Preferences in a Desegregated School: A Round Robin Analysis," *Journal of Personality and Social Psychology*, Vol. 46, No. 4, 1984, pp. 799–810.

Williams, Christopher W., Richard S. Brown, Paul R. Lees-Haley, and J. Randall Price, "An Attributional (Causal Dimensional) Analysis of Perceptions of Sexual Harassment," *Journal of Applied Social Psychology*, Vol. 25, No. 13, July 1–15, 1995, pp. 1169–1183.

Zweigenhaft, Richard L., and G. William Domhoff, *Blacks in the White Establishment? A Study of Race and Class in America*, New Haven and London: Yale University Press, 1991.